Digging Deep

Also Available in the Moving Middle Schools Series

More Than the Truth
Teaching Nonfiction Writing Through Journalism

Through Mathematical Eyes
Exploring Functional Relationships in Math and Science

Digging Deep

Teaching Social Studies Through the Study of Archaeology

Edited by

Dennie Palmer Wolf

Dana Balick

Julie Craven

Heinemann
Portsmouth, NH

Heinemann
A division of Reed Elsevier Inc.
361 Hanover Street
Portsmouth, NH 03801-3912
Offices and agents throughout the world

Library of Congress Cataloging-in-Publication Data
Digging deep : teaching social studies through the study of
   archaeology / edited by Dennie Palmer Wolf, Dana Balick, and Julie
   Craven.
      p.   cm.—(Moving middle schools)
   Includes bibliographical references (p. 144).
   ISBN 0-435-07218-8 (paper)
   1. Archaeology—Study and teaching (Middle school)
   2. Civilization, Ancient—Study and teaching (Middle school)
   3. World history—Study and teaching (Middle school)   I. Wolf,
   Dennie.   II. Balick, Dana.   III. Craven, Julie.   IV. Series.
   CC83.D87   1997
   930.1'0712—dc21   97-30030
                                                              CIP

Consulting editor: Maureen Barbieri
Production editor: Elizabeth Valway
Cover illustration: Joseph Jones
Cover designer: Jenny Jensen Greenleaf
Manufacturing coordinator: Louise Richardson

Printed in the United States of America on acid-free paper
01 00 99 98 97   RRD   1 2 3 4 5 6

Contents

Foreword: About This Series and Volume   vii
Dennie Palmer Wolf

Acknowledgments   xix

Introduction
Archaeology and Cultural Exploration
William A. Saturno and Dennie Palmer Wolf   1

Prologue to Chapter 1
The Eagle and the Tortoise: A Colleague's Tale
Nick Bartel   24

1 You Are Here
A Cultural Exploration of the Maya and Seventh Graders
Marg Costello   29

Response from a Colleague: Creating a Culture of Respect
Bill Fulton   52

2 We Knew Where We Wanted to Go and We Think
We May Have Arrived
Phyllis McDonough Rado and Victoria Rodríguez Garvey   58

Response from a Colleague
Virginia Vogel Zanger   84

3 Like a Puzzle   90
Tammy Swales Metzler

Response from a Colleague: Closing the Gap by
Beginning at the End
Chris Hargrave   109

4 "More of a Questioning Spirit"
Unearthing Ancient Greece
Miriam Nason and Shannon Thomas   112

Response from a Colleague
Dennie Palmer Wolf   130

Epilogue
But I Don't Teach the Maya . . .   135
Julie Craven

Appendix: Maya Adult Bibliography   144

Contributors   **156**

Foreword: About This Series and Volume

About This Series

Beginning in 1991 with a grant from the Rockefeller Foundation, PACE, an unusual collaborative of urban educators, got under way. In six sites across the country (Fort Worth, Texas; Pittsburgh, Pennsylvania; Rochester, New York; San Diego and San Francisco, California; and Wilmington, Delaware), teams of teachers began creating "portfolio cultures"—classrooms that emphasize growth toward high common standards, as well as reflection for both students and teachers. The image of a classroom as a culture where a complex network of daily actions supports thinking and imagination provides an important tool for rethinking not just assessment, but curriculum, teaching, and connections to families and surrounding communities.

It was no accident that this work was centered in middle schools. Early adolescence is one of the most promising and most vulnerable moments in the life span of young Americans. Contrary to our stereotypical views of adolescents, many students between the ages of ten and fifteen have their eyes intensely focused on the world "out there." They want to know, "What kind of place is there for me—and others like me?" When the answer is harsh and discouraging, we see cynicism, doubt, and disengagement. When the answer is honest and makes a place for young people to invest in modern urban life, we get back humor and fantasy, invention and insight, humility and curiosity.

Early on in our work of creating portfolio cultures, we began to question the usual proposition that "as soon as schools are orderly, safe, and respectful, we will be able to launch new kinds of learning." Absolutely true, in one sense: neither teachers nor students can learn in danger. But one day, as we looked at the costs of installing metal detectors in all of one city's middle schools, a teacher and a central office administrator brought a question to the larger group: "Couldn't it be that once learning is under way, then we will see orderly, safe, and respectful schools?" In the wake of that startling reversal, we began to think about the major learning challenges that young adolescents could take on and enjoy—which could make it possible for many more of them to travel from elementary to high school thinking of themselves as authors, scientists, historians, artists, and mathematicians.

In that process, we developed a unique way of working together that we have come to call "curriculum seminars." The seminars are a series of professional development experiences geared to supporting teachers in developing those major learning challenges. Identifying what those challenges are did not happen overnight. We spent almost two years in middle schools across the nation, a world of almost wild contrasts. In some settings, students wrote, did research, and investigated mathematical regularities in the natural world. Elsewhere the curriculum was stagnant; as one student commented, "I did the work of a third grader for three years." We also knew that in a number of settings the original imperative for creating a special kind of learning environment between elementary and high schools had dwindled to a series of gimmicks: posters for book reports, math "problems of the week" that were actually endless calculations, word searches for science vocabulary, models of the universe made from gumdrops, or computer games masquerading as historical simulations.

We knew that middle school was three years that most students—especially those in city schools—did not have to waste. Working in the strongest middle schools in the six sites that we had chosen, we began a series of interviews during which we asked experienced middle school teachers to think out loud about the major learning tasks of middle school. The tasks we were looking for had two characteristics. First, students who mastered these tasks demonstrated understandings that "made all the difference"; they were no longer kids, but young adults. One teacher called these lessons "the rod and the staff" or "the sword and buckler" of learning. Another suggested that we think about them as similar to the invention of the microscope or the advent of movable type: "small revolutions of the mind and heart."

Second, these tasks encapsulated understandings that were hard to teach. If we were honest with one another, we had to admit that they were especially hard to teach to students who "didn't either arrive already knowing them, or at least being close to it." And if we were out-and-out blunt, we would admit that we rarely managed to confer these capacities on the students who depended on school the most: those whose families and life circumstances could not supply these understandings.

In addition to our interviews, we asked teachers to look at collections of student work from their own and other sites to identify evidence of these understandings—or the lack thereof. We had further conversations, observed in their classes, and spoke to the high school teachers who received their students. The consensus was strong across disciplines. Once we boiled it down, the list was short. Teachers wanted students to be able to do the following:

- write powerful nonfiction
- bridge from the concrete work of arithmetic to the conceptual and formal world of mathematics that permits modeling and prediction
- use multiple sources, especially primary sources, as evidence to piece together a larger whole, such as hypothesis and research, an investigation, or an argument
- create an original work—for instance, a series of poems, a story, or a theatrical or musical performance—with some grace and humanity, polished through the use of research, consultation with others, and revision.

Fine, but then what? We had to find a way to turn research into action. The first step was to search for the kinds of enterprises that could embody these understandings so as to make them teachable. Many twists and turns later, we came up with journalism, science investigations that employed mathematics to capture regularities, archaeology, and the collaborative work of a company of artists such as those who bring an opera, a museum exhibition, or a new edition of poetry to fruition.

Using these enterprises as working models, we asked teachers in the PACE network if they would become involved in a two-year process to develop curriculum that would make these major understandings available to a full range of learners. These became our curriculum seminars. Over the course of the next three years we, teachers, researchers, and outside experts, worked together.

- We used portfolios of work from both struggling and accomplished students to investigate what prevents many students from being successful at gaining major understandings.
- We took on the role of novice learners in immersion experiences that took us deep into the workrooms and thoughts of adults whose life work depends on these understandings—journalists, scientists, archaeologists, musicians, and artists. This took us to the city to practice journalism, into a collaboration with scientists and mathematicians, to a museum to look at the artifacts of Mayan civilization, and ultimately into settings where artists collaborated.
- We designed and drafted curricula to make these big ideas and powerful strategies available to students.
- We taught those curricula and brought the evidence of student work back to the seminar for help, information, and critique.
- We revised and retaught the curricula.
- We thought about the resulting student work in the light of demanding performance standards.
- We reflected on what we had learned.
- We presented and published what we knew from our work together.

In the last step, teachers once again stepped outside their classrooms, this time to become authors. The chapters here are their reflections on what is possible for young adolescent learners—no matter what their history, income, country of origin, or first language. What emerged was not only the manuscript that has now become this book but a new vision of accomplished and experienced teachers' work. The PACE teachers, who had also become researchers and authors, insisted that this kind of hybrid between intense classroom engagement and adult reflection was something they never again wanted to be without.

But like all long-term human endeavors, the "last" step is never really the last. Once we completed the first two books of the series (*More than the Truth*, about students learning journalism, and *Through Mathematical Eyes*, a look at students learning about functions in math and science), we realized that we had made a huge mistake. We were writing about students, but we never bothered to ask them if we had got the story straight. It was as if we had written the experiment and then simply allowed them to do the measuring, the heating, and the washing up of glassware.

So, in putting together this volume, teachers and researchers have worked closely with students. In some classrooms, students acted as local ethnographers, sending us messages about what they observed happening in their classrooms. Using email to respond, we built a shared conversation about learning as it occurred. In other classrooms, students helped out by participating in interviews at the beginning and the conclusion of their work. Many of the most insightful comments on learning found in these chapters emerged from those conversations. Finally, and admittedly with the trepidation that comes when you ask your most important and toughest critics for their opinions, we have asked students to be our first line of editors. Working with teachers' first drafts, PACE researchers edited the manuscripts, inserting questions and comments where we needed students' answers. Sometimes those replies came winging to us via email. But elsewhere, teachers and students organized the equivalent of Socratic seminars; the seminal work at the center of the discussion was the manuscript describing what they had learned. The result, we believe, is a much livelier manuscript, chock full of students' commentary. In the process, we believe that we have uncovered yet another corner of educational work that can be opened up to joint discussion. At one time, we thought that our only responsibility after asking to use students' work was to find the dollars to give every student a copy of the book that contained it. Now, we have come to understand that although that's fine, the real goal is to issue a "come one, come all" invitation for students to join in as authors and critics.

But, as any reader knows, the genuinely last step of this work doesn't belong to us. It's yours. You and your colleagues, be they fellow teachers or students, will read and reflect, implement and revise what you find between these covers. So be it, so long as growing numbers of students have the chance to engage, invent, and understand.

About This Volume

The following is a description of one of my visits to a seventh-grade class in Texas.

Late in the afternoon, when the fall is still warmer than it is supposed to be, even here in Texas, the students are working on the section of their social studies textbook about the Native American tribes of the region. Earlier in the week they each chose a tribe to study. Today in class they are asked to find the section of the book on their tribe, read it, and write down questions about what they still want to know.

When the heavy covers flop open to the wide glossy pages, this is what they meet:

> The Coahuiltecans seldom strayed from the dry and brushy land called the South Texas Plain. Coahuiltecans hunted javelina, deer, and bison with bows and arrows and also foraged. They gathered and dried cactus, mesquite, afave, and other plants and ground them into flour. When game was scarce, they ate worms, lizards, and plants. Constantly on the move to find food, Coahuiltecans seldom spent more than a few weeks at each campsite.
>
> All members of Coahuiltecan society were equal and shared whatever food and water they had. In camp, everyone had work to do. Women took care of the camp while men hunted. Those who were unable or too old to do the heavy work still worked at other tasks. Shamans were important to

Coahuiltecan life just as they were to other Native American peoples. Shamans led the religious ceremonies, made medicine from plants, herbs, and berries, and cared for the sick.

By the time Texas became part of the United States, the Coahuiltecans had all but disappeared from the Gulf region. Many were killed in battle with Apaches and Comanches. Others had moved into Mexico or into other areas. A great many Coahuiltecans died from diseases that the Europeans brought to the region. (*Texas and Texans*, Adrian N. Anderson [et al.] Lake Forest, IL: Glencoe, 1993, p. 107).

These passages encapsulate stretches of human life like a prairie; nothing is stirring. It is a world strangely without motive or consequence, an account where migration, loss, and brutal change just happen like the ordinary procession of days.

A student I am sitting with scavenges for his pencil, runs his finger under the sentences about foodstuffs and hunting, and writes out his questions in soft lead letters:

What kind of food did they eat?
What did they hunt with?
What did they use to make flour?

Mrs. Richardson circulates through the room, looking over the kids' shoulders and working with them on their questions. She stops by one young man, reads over his shoulder, and then wags her finger at him, funny and dead serious at once: "Charles, you did your slick thing here. Someone, sometime, taught you how to turn a sentence into a question. You think I am going to take this? What do you think, you think I'm dead? I don't think so. Not yet anyway. You can't slide this by me. You're gonna get a second chance." She turns the paper over and points to it, meaning business.

Facing the class, she says, "You all, don't you think that I want that kind of question. I can read it in my book all by myself. Don't think I can't tell the difference."

Later on, Charles hands the paper back to Mrs. Richardson with a new set of questions.

Did they move from place to place?
Did they have a government?

She rests her hand on his shoulder, as if he were a local hero, and speaks just loud enough so all of us can hear about his resurrection: "Charles, you restored my faith. I knew you could write a real question if you tried. Now I don't want to see another of those book questions. Just brain questions, you hear? So, let's us make this one a real brain question. Assume they had a government. They were a big group of people that had to keep order, so of course they had a government. Now what do you really want to be asking?"

Charles says, "Like, what kind of government did they have? Did they have to have police?"

Mrs. Richardson tries her hand. "Well, what about how they enforced their laws? Is that it?" A few minutes later she is back, looking down at his next questions:

Did they have education?
Did they have a lot of people?

"What do you mean?" she asks.

"Did they go to school? Like, did they read and write?" he says, half guessing, since this "real question" business is new—kind of like a newly waxed floor, something you are drawn to but aren't quite sure you want to tread on.

"So, do you want to know about their formal education system? What about it?"

"Did they read and write?"

"Okay, but they also had other kinds of education. They taught their children to hunt, what to believe about the world, how to grow crops. So you need to know what part of their education system you want to know about. And you need to be able to say why that question is important. What are you going to know that matters when you have the answer?"

Mrs. Richardson stands in the middle of the class, her hand still on Charles's shoulder. She has that look of a person about to say something large. "Look, you all, we are not just looking for something you can put in a report, get a check, and be done with it. We are looking for things you want to know. And don't just be leaving them in the past. They go on, you know. My mother was half Cherokee. She wasn't raised by them, because she was adopted by other people, but if you saw her, you could tell right away. So think about them as living people who have to get along today, too. Just like all the rest of us."

They write and she moves among them, probing and joking, returning to see that they have taken their questions one step further each time she swings by. "Okay, now I want you to write down what steps you need to take if you are going to find the answers to these questions. I tried getting us time in the library and that was a big flop. But we aren't stopping there. So I want you to write down whatever you think it is going to take to get you those answers. Do you want me to get you out a stack of books? What do we need to watch? Put down your wildest dreams. If you want to have a Native American come in here to talk with us, you put it down. It might happen."

Mrs. Richardson is wrestling with the demons at the end of the chapter. There, for as long as they have been in school, Charles and all the rest of her students have learned about other cultures and different times through commands like:

> "Name three of the Native American nations of the Southeastern culture."
> "Explain how the Native American cultures within Texas depended on their environment and natural resources."
> "Make a chart about four different Native American cultures, using these topics: the location of their culture; the way the culture obtained food, weapons, tools, and clothing; and their form of government and social structure."

But Mrs. Richardson is having none of it, nor is she about to be stopped dead in her tracks by any unwilling school librarian. If her students learn that a question is something they want to know, rather than something they fill in at the end of the chapter, then she is there to joke with them, insist on thinking, get books, and put her own history on the table.

This is a book about taking on the back-of-the-chapter demons —and winning. It tells the story of a network of middle school social studies teachers who tamed their centuries-long, civilizations-packed courses in world history and culture by turning them into inquiries informed by the questions and tools of archaeology.

In the opening chapter, William A. Saturno, an archaeologist who studies Mayan civilization in Honduras, introduces the major dimensions of archaeological work. He highlights the central place of questions, evidence, and most importantly, inference: the work of digging deep. But *digging deep* has another meaning as well. Saturno makes the point that no investigation of another culture should go forward without our digging deep within ourselves to locate a curiosity tempered by both humanity (the Maya are the sum of their experiences, not their monuments and rituals) and humility (we will understand the Maya only gradually, partially, and in a way that requires ongoing revision).

In the early chapters, a group of teachers describe three versions of digging deep, using the core example of teaching their students about Mayan civilization. Marg Costello, working with Nick Bartel, describes her work in which she actively connects the world of the ancient Maya with the contemporary world of Central American politics and learning which is rooted in community service. Threading throughout her work is the conviction that the Mayas' struggle to survive and preserve their centuries-old languages and culture carries vital messages for her seventh graders about persistence and resilience.

In the second chapter, Phyllis McDonough Rado and Victoria Rodríguez Garvey explain how they used the study of Mayan civilization as a major tool for integrating their school's mainstream and bilingual populations. To hear their bilingual students give firsthand accounts of archaeologists at work, translate materials available only in Spanish, and argue for bilingual editions of students' Mayan folktales is to see an American education where several languages, not only English, are understood to be avenues for understanding.

Using the framework of Gardner's multiple intelligences, Tammy Swales Metzler convinces her seventh graders to regard the many forms of Mayan thought, rather than monumental pyramids or ritual sacrifices, as the heartbeat of the culture. Her culminating event—a conference during which each student speaks as an expert on the nature of and evidence for Mayan thought—provides a compelling example of how an extremely clear vision of a final performance can inform every step of the teaching leading up to it.

In Chapter Four, teachers Miriam Nason and Shannon Thomas demonstrate how this same archaeological framework can be applied to other civilizations. They describe an exploration of ancient Greece that couples a computer simulation of a dig with an equally intensive investigation of what Greek writers, philosophers, and scientists have to teach us about the importance of asking questions and our responsibilities as citizens and thinkers to answer those questions to the best of our abilities.

Stilley leads us into her science classroom where student archaeologists decode a find of Native American artifacts, using the tools of mathematics and science.

Taking a step back from the classroom, Julie Craven closes the volume by thinking aloud about what we have learned about professional development with—not *for*—teachers in the three years that we have pursued this work. She speaks to these possibilities as a teacher who has applied the lessons of the curriculum seminar to units on the civil rights movement and China.

The lessons are ones of exhilaration and enactment. It is exhilarating to decode Mayan glyphs and build theories about Mayan cities from aerial photographs of ruins. Knowing means you have something to teach. But just as intellectually arousing are the questions of enactment. Much like athletes or musicians, teachers have to embody or enact their understanding so that it becomes both clear and irresistible for students. This cannot be left to teachers' manuals or preprofessional courses.

A number of the teachers have joked—in that very serious way that we use humor to raise the most difficult issues we face—about the "interdisciplinary" or "crosscultural scars" they have earned in this process. The way is mostly uncharted, so we learn by lurching in the dark, bumping into things. But at the end of our three years of working together, we could make an amulet to hang about the neck of anyone who is willing to walk the path. On this amulet might be written questions for all those who want to use archaeology as their framework:

> Are you willing to work by question and evidence, not question and answer?
> Will you persevere long enough for understanding to develop?
> Can you work from firsthand materials?
> Can you interview an artifact? Read a mural? Work with documents?
> Do you have literature from the culture—not just historical fiction where the culture provides an exotic backdrop?
> Have you partners who know the culture from the inside out?

On the reverse side of this amulet, we would imprint questions for those who see archaeological work as the ideal place to do cross-disciplinary work:

> Is this unit/project a genuine partnership or a thematic confection?
> Are worthwhile understandings being taught in each discipline, or is one being turned into a handmaiden?
> If a biologist, mathematician, artist, or historian walked by the room and eavesdropped, would s/he say, "There is some elegant science, mathematics, art, or history going on in there"?
> Do these disciplines come together in this way anywhere else? In later studies? In the world of work?

Perhaps this only sounds cryptic. But once you have read the chapters, these messages will read much more like watchwords of a faith. We offer them to Mrs. Richardson, in every classroom where she teaches, in every state of the Union.

Acknowledgments

This series, Moving Middle Schools, is the result of many people joining together and buckling down. We want to begin by thanking the author-teachers who were willing to venture into what was to be a mix of teaching, researching, writing, and collegial exchange. They signed up without a recipe, participated in seminars with strangers, taught using unforeseen methods, and reflected on their work by writing after school and into the nights. Behind the teachers are the colleagues and principals who covered classes, read drafts, and made exceptions. Behind those educators are the urban districts that worked with us to endorse serious school reform: Fort Worth, Texas; Pittsburgh, Pennsylvania; Rochester, New York; San Diego and San Francisco, California; and Wilmington, Delaware. We also want to thank the students who made these projects possible. They gave generously of their time, their thoughts, and their writing. They, too, were without a blueprint. Just back of the students are families who stayed up to proofread, went to the library one more time, attended field trips, or answered interview questions when they could have gone out, read, napped, or eaten supper.

We also owe thanks to another set of "critical friends"—people who worked along with us, even as they asked difficult questions and set unforgivingly high standards: Edmund Gordon, Carol Bonilla-Bowman, Melissa Lemons, and Patty Taylor. For this volume, we are indebted to the Peabody Museum of Archaeology and Ethnology at Harvard University; Marion Wingfield, Manager of Education Programs for the museum's department; Roxanne Reddington-Wilde, Museum Educator; and Bill Saturno, Mayanist, for their generous giving of expertise and time in the planning and execution of our Maya Curriculum Seminars. Most recently, we are indebted to the editors and staff of Heinemann publishers, who were willing to work with us, even though we were, and remain, a collaborative, with all the varied ideas and voices that term implies.

Finally, we want to thank those who, as many as five years ago, were willing to support research on school reform in urban settings. This work grew to become PACE (Performance Assessment Collaboratives for Education), a network of urban school districts committed to high standards of practice for students, teachers, and schools that historically have not experienced sustained support and abundant resources. PACE invented the curriculum seminars that, in turn, gave birth to this series of books. That original generosity—in particular, the willingness to provide a rare five years of work together—has made us remember that the first meaning of the word *foundation* is a solid footing on which a structure can be built. So we thank Alberta Arthurs, Hugh Price, Jamie Jensen, and Marla Ucelli at the Rockefeller Foundation, and Warren Simmons and Lynn White at the Annie E. Casey Foundation.

Introduction

Archaeology and Cultural Exploration

William A. Saturno and Dennie Palmer Wolf

As a child, I loved dirt. At times there was no separating me from it. The small "diggin' hole" in the backyard of my childhood home in upstate New York captivated me. Its crabgrass and wild strawberries held endless curiosities: potato bugs, toys buried and long forgotten, old bottle caps, and spoons bent and twisted from prior excavations. Yet for me it was more than just a dusty repository for discarded artifacts; it was a cauldron for my imagination. In Albany's museum, mummies extracted from the sands in Egypt and mastodons uncovered in New York's own muddy loam stood as evidence of the great wealth hidden beneath the topsoil. My backyard's clay certainly held similar treasures: if not an ancient civilization or extinct beast, then perhaps an arrowhead, or maybe a passage to the earth's core. Fueled by both knowledge and fantasy, I persisted in my hopeful quarrying. I never did find much in that hole that I hadn't buried there myself, but in my boyhood dreams, I was an archaeologist.

However, boyhood dreams are often short-lived, and mine were no different. It wasn't long before I wanted to be Batman or Captain Kirk instead of Howard Carter (the discoverer of Tut's tomb), and my diggin' hole returned completely to the crabgrass. School did little to rekindle my interest. Rather, it directed me toward math and science, which occupied my imagination just as well. Thus, as I progressed through my education, I continued to concentrate on math and science; archaeology became more a part of my remote personal history than a possible career. It surfaced only

1

in conversations about what I wanted to be when I was "a little kid," and even then it was not an example that I, or anyone else, took very seriously.

Now, as I write from the jungles of Central America, it is clear that the dirt from my childhood never fully came out from under my fingernails. From the very beginning, archaeology has opened my eyes to new worlds: from the fantasy worlds of mummies and mastodons in my youth, to the tropical worlds of Mayan ruins in my adulthood. Through the archaeological study of people, past and present, I have gained a deep respect for other cultures. It is this respect more than anything else that I wish to pass on. Teaching archaeology to students can do that.

Respecting other ways of life demands understanding. Understanding, however, is very different from a simple knowledge of raw facts, such as, "Classic Mayan civilization began in A.D. 250 and lasted until A.D. 850." It is also different from the compilations of idiosyncrasies that have often passed as world history. "Did you know that the Quechua of South America eat their potatoes covered with *mud*?" Or, "Can you believe the Maya deformed their children's *heads*?" Using these exotic details to discuss societies generally conveys, frequently unintentionally, the unfortunate notion that anything different from the way *we* do things is somewhat ridiculous. In this way, exercises in cultural exploration have often hindered the understanding they sought to instill.

This volume is intended as a "backpacker's guide" to the exploration and understanding of other cultures in schools. As such, it provides only a framework for exploration, pointing out some of the best trails and most common pitfalls. Like a backpacking trip, the journey into another culture will always be a personal experience. Everyone brings slightly different equipment for the trek, and everyone takes home a slightly different memory of the adventure. Certain tools, however, can help anyone to make the trip more easily—a map, for example. Archaeology can be one of these tools. However, before we can use archaeology as a tool, several persistent misconceptions must first be cleared away.

If you were to ask someone what an archaeologist looks like, invariably one of a few images would spring to mind. The most common is that of Indiana Jones. This character, brought to life on the big screen by Harrison Ford, has become inextricably married to the public conception of archaeology. Other images from popular Western culture do little to clarify the archaeologist's role. Whether exposed to a scene from *Abbott and Costello Meet the Mummy* or a documentary on "the lost city of Atlantis," people are constantly being misguided about what archaeologists do and what archaeology is. Archaeology is not about the high adventure of the mummy's curse. It's about scientific inquiry and research.

Archaeology, as defined by Webster's Dictionary, is the scientific study of material remains (like fossil relics, artifacts, and monuments) of past human life and activities. It is derived from two Greek words: *logia*, meaning "the study of," and *archaio-* meaning "something old," such as pot shards, sarcophagi, lost temples, or skeletons. However, neither the definition nor its roots illuminate the real focus of archaeological study: people. Archaeology is, in fact, a subfield of anthropology, the study of humans. So although it is true that archaeologists study the material remains of past human activities, it is the activities and the people behind them, not the objects, that we seek to understand. The objects are simply clues to understanding past human lifeways.

Another misconception about the nature of archaeological inquiry is how long ago these activities must have taken place in order to be fit for study. People commonly think of archaeology as dealing solely with ancient civilizations or the Stone Age, and although this notion serves to stimulate interest in the field, it simultaneously detracts from its relevance. Archaeology is about understanding patterns of living; thus, the same exact techniques that permit archaeologists to investigate how the Peruvian Ice Maiden died can be applied to what happened yesterday. Although it's true that some archaeologists travel to remote regions of the world to investigate the ruins of ancient cities like Machu Picchu or Angkor Wat, others deal with more contemporary topics. There are archaeologists who study the garbage our society produces and the formation of landfills. There are archaeologists who study the patterns of remains left at crime scenes and the forensic remains of crime victims. In short, to be a valid subject of archaeological investigation, the remains need not be old; they need simply be the results of human actions. Defined in this way, archaeology is about our ability to draw thoughtful inferences based on the remains of human activity and our own knowledge of human experience. Archaeology is not a set of technical and historical skills needed only by those trying to unlock ancient mysteries; it is a set of necessary skills that we all use.

A working mother of a middle-school-aged child arrives home from work around 4:00 P.M. She is frantic: her child is not at the neighbors'. But when she enters the house, she sees her child's jacket draped over a kitchen chair. There is a pile of books on the counter near a ceramic jar with the lid unseated slightly. There is a glass in the sink with crumbs clinging to its inside wall and a thin white film at its bottom. It is not difficult for the mother to reconstruct the events leading to the current state of the remains found in her kitchen. Her child arrived home, discarded the jacket, and set down the books on the counter. He/she opened the cookie jar and failed to replace the top exactly as it had been. He/she filled the glass with milk and proceeded to dunk the cookies into the glass, leaving crumbs suspended in the liquid. When the milk was finally drunk the few crumbs that remained were stranded on the glass' inner wall. The glass was then placed unrinsed into the sink, and the child went about his/her business. The mother can also assume that since his/her books are still on the counter, no homework has yet been done.

The remains conform to a pattern of behavior with which the mother is familiar. Perhaps it is not the first time she has returned home to find her kitchen as described. Perhaps she herself has at some time left a similar arrangement of artifacts. If the pattern of the remains in the story above held meaning for you, if you, too, were able to discern the activities that produced them, it is because of your own cultural experience. If you found a similar pattern of remains in an archaeological excavation of a room in a nineteenth-century brownstone in Boston's Back Bay, you might draw a similar conclusion about the chain of events that left the artifacts where they lie. This conclusion could not be drawn from your cultural experience and the artifact assemblage alone, but rather in conjunction with your understanding of nineteenth-century Boston culture as being closely related to your own.

However, if the culture that deposited the artifacts had neither cookies nor milk you would have to alter your hypotheses considerably. You would need to form new hypotheses based on the objects you knew that culture had. For example, if that culture made ceramics glazed with a thin white slip glaze, we could hypothesize that the white residue at the bottom of the glass might be the remains of the glaze. Likewise, what you thought were crumbs clinging to the side of the glass could be the grit that was mixed into the glaze after the glaze had been mixed.

That similar patterns of remains can be left by very different activities poses some interesting problems for the archaeologist. We can never *know* exactly what happened in the past. We can only test hypotheses and arrive at the most likely situation, given all the information at hand. The above example can be boiled down to four core skills that are at the heart of archaeological study:

1. genuine curiosity
2. careful inquiry
3. thoughtful inference
4. humility

By using these core skills in schools, we can transform the social studies or world history classroom.

Genuine Curiosity

When world history is taught in middle school, it risks being presented as a series of "just so" stories of what happened in the past. Whether the unit is about Dynastic Egypt or Imperial Rome or Classic Maya Kingdoms, students are often given histories and cultures as a series of names, places, and events. All of this information is presented as fact, things we as teachers know and they as students must learn. This type of presentation can be stale. In order to add life to these presentations and to spark interest in the subject matter, teachers usually rely on the exoticness of the culture being studied. In this format, cultures are generally discussed as either "surprisingly advanced" or "very mysterious," if not both. "Isn't it amazing that the Egyptians could have built the pyramids with the limited technology at their disposal?" "How could the Maya construct great cities in the rain forest and then disappear without a trace?" Exercises of this type, which focus on the improbability of a culture's accomplishments, rarely lead to the understanding of another culture. For example, extraterrestrial influence has continually and unfortunately surfaced as an answer to both the above questions—an answer that gives little insight into the cultures being studied. Archaeology, however, can provide a more dynamic framework for cultural exploration that generates interest based on their experience and active participation in the discovery process, rather than on the "surprising" sophistication or "mystery" of the culture being studied.

Careful Inquiry

By giving students an account of a culture's material remains and their context, students themselves can begin to form ideas and hypotheses about that culture's way of life. These hypotheses can be constantly tested and refined by the inclusion of more data from ever-broadening contexts. Students can begin to deal with the tension between finding a pattern in the evidence they have pieced together and forcing one upon it. In this way, they can begin to uncover the history of a culture rather than simply read or hear about it as fact.

Thoughtful Inference

Archaeological study is in large part the assembly of an enormous cultural puzzle. A culture's architecture, art, artifacts, historical records, mythology, and folklore are all pieces. However, we as archaeologists have no puzzle box top. We cannot know for certain exactly how the myriad pieces fit together; rather, we must strive to find the best fit. To build the puzzle we must rely not only on the evidence collected through our careful inquiry, but we must draw thoughtful inferences from it. We must call upon our own knowledge of human experience, as we did with the cookies and milk, while remaining somewhat skeptical of our results. If we were to find wool garments, would that necessarily mean that sheep were kept in that culture? Couldn't it just as easily mean that they traded with people who kept sheep? As part of this process, the picture that we see is always changing. We must constantly be looking for new pieces to clarify our picture. If we were to find the tools used to transform raw wool into cloth, or the skeletal remains of large numbers of sheep, how would that change our picture? Students in middle school classrooms can use archaeology to enable them to go beyond mere acquisition of historical facts and into the process of cultural exploration.

Humility Being Humble

Knowing the limits of one's own experience is an invaluable skill for the archaeologist. In Western society, life is often considered in economic terms. People are generally thought of as economically rational—that is, they attempt to be as efficient as possible to obtain a desired end. If you wish to catch the train from Boston to Chicago, you will not likely choose one that goes via Houston. However, other cultures in the world do not act strictly in economic terms. The Zapotec of both ancient and modern-day Mexico practice a form of agriculture in which the goal is not to maximize their crop yield but rather to grow just enough food, no more, no less. Their goal of not creating a surplus may be quite foreign to us, but it is nonetheless a genuine guiding force in their culture. Thus, it is important to be humble when drawing inferences about a culture. An archaeologist's goal is to understand a culture framed in its own terms.

With these issues in hand, I want to turn away from archaeology as a way of knowing, to archaeology as a way of teaching. I want to share what I see as three essential elements: the work of choosing an entry point, the necessity of building up a fund of knowledge, and the pleasures of digging deep.

Choosing an Entry Point: Making a Gateway to Understanding

Many great cities—ancient, medieval, and Renaissance—had magnificent gates. Before you could enter Great Zimbabwe, Troy, or Florence, you had to pass through a giant and elaborate portal. Yes, those gates were certainly for protection, and sometimes for taxation, but they also signaled to any traveler: "Behold! You are about to enter a great work of many hands, a capital of human enterprise and imagination."

As teachers, we ought to remember those fabulous gateways. How we begin matters. When choosing a point of entry into another culture, it is important that it not be too intimidating. A good entrance should have the universal appeal that even a novice can appreciate, while at the same time providing a clear path to other, deeper avenues of cultural exploration. And, not insignificantly, whatever that entry point is, it should signal that the hard work of gathering and making sense of information is exhilarating, not deadly.

For example, Chinese culture might be entered through a unit on its cuisine. This is not to suggest that by going to a Chinese restaurant one gains access to the entire wealth of Chinese culture and history, but that the potential for an entry is there. Most people are familiar with Chinese food of some form. Learning something about the traditions and preparations involved in the development of Chinese cuisine can provide a base for later discussions of Chinese agriculture, economy, or political and cultural divisions. When exploring a culture with which students or teachers have had little or no contact, a comfortable point of entry is even more important. Don't bite off too much at once. Rather, it is necessary to ease into another culture to avoid overemphasizing the ways *they* are different from *us*.

The curriculum seminar in Mayan culture that I participated in is a case in point. Many heads were involved in its design: Marion Wingfield, director of education at the Peabody Museum of Archaeology and Ethnology at Harvard University; Roxanne Reddington, a graduate student in the department of Celtic Studies and student of archaeology; myself; and the PACE researchers. We had two days to launch what was going to be a several-year endeavor to develop curriculum on the Maya of Mexico and Central America, a complex culture with both ancient and modern components and many lessons to teach about the art of exploring a civilization different from our own. The Maya, in the centuries preceding the beginning of the Christian era (B.C.E.), developed an artistically elaborate, sociopolitically complex, and regionally heterogeneous civilization. The descendants of this ancient civilization, more than four million in Guatemala alone, still reside in the same region. Many continue to practice traditional lifeways; others have been acculturated into Central America's industrialized world system, while still others strike a delicate balance between the two. The information available to those who wish to study the Maya is immense and multifaceted. At our disposal are the records of more than one hundred years of archaeological excavations, as well as the written records of Spanish chroniclers of the colonial period and ethnographers of the present day. We can examine the current writings of modern Maya scholars, and with the recent decipherment of Maya hieroglyphic script, we can draw as well upon the information recorded in stone, pottery, and bark paper books by the ancient Maya. In short, there is a vast array of data to draw upon. But for me—just like for any other teacher—the question was where to begin, what path to take, and with what end in mind.

The entry point we chose for the seminar was Mayan mathematics, specifically, their numerical system. This is by no means the only possible starting point, but I thought then and still think it is the most elegant one. Mathematics and counting are universal; all cultures have some system of accounting, whether they are counting the days until the rainy season begins or the number of roots they have stored for the winter. The Maya, however, are one of the few cultures in the history of the world—along with the Arabs, Romans, and Chinese—who developed a system to record their counts in writing. The Mayan system is simple in that it represents numerical values of infinite size with only three basic symbols. Our own numerical system, derived from that of the Arabs, uses ten symbols to accomplish the same task. Because the system has only three symbols, its code was easily cracked. The Mayan number system was one of the first breakthroughs in deciphering Maya hieroglyphics. As such, it provides not only an appropriate road into Maya culture, one that teachers and students can relate to, but one that reflects the historical path that professional archaeologists have taken.

Once we gathered in what was to be our work room at the Peabody Museum, everyone was asked to decipher a problem that the museum's education department had designed, essentially a series of Maya numbers—that is, a combination of dots, dashes, and shells. (See Introduction Figures 1 and 2.)

Teachers and researchers alike all gazed at the bars and dots in front of them and began their archaeological journey. For some, patterns emerged almost immediately: "In any given number, there is never a string of dots longer than four." "The largest cluster of symbols is always three bars and four dots."

From this data the teachers quickly began to draw inferences: "The dots are equal to one." "Since with dots alone you can't count past four, the bars are equal to five." "So the largest number must be equal to 19, since it is 3 bars, which is 3x5, plus 4 dots, which is 4x1."

Based on their newly minted hypotheses, I offered everyone a series of more complex numbers to decipher. (See Introduction Figure 3.) They identified a third symbol, a shell, which they designated a place holder or zero. They calculated the values of the various place values in Mayan numbers: ones, twenties (20 × 1), four-hundreds (20 × 20), eight-thousands (20 × 400), etc. They then discussed how a base 20 system might have developed. Right away someone pointed out that we all have twenty fingers and toes. End of discussion. Things were moving fast. In part, this was because everyone could contribute to solving a human puzzle that was challenging—but not impossible—given their knowledge of how cultures and minds work. Had I lectured on the "Evolution of Vegesimal (base 20) Counting Systems in Preclassical Mayan Cultures," they might well have been yawning or wondering where the famous bookstores of Cambridge could be found. Instead, we were jointly examining the same data (bars, dots, and shells) that

INTRODUCTION FIGURE 1.

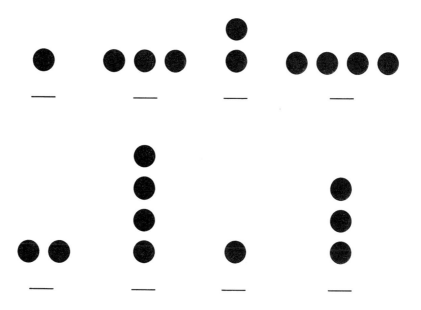

*Time for some fun! After getting off the plane and settling in, you spent yesterday discovering the wonders of the market the contemporary Maya hold in town. Today, you go out into the jungle, exploring the ruins of an ancient Maya city. These people have been here more than a thousand years. Clambering over the tumbled stone slabs, you notice that they are carved. Certain shapes repeat again and again. They are distinct, round dots. Often, but not always, the **dots** are accompanied by a bar under them. The bars occasionally appear alone, too. Sometimes, the dots and bars appear in clusters. Other complicated designs appear around them, but there is no clear pattern of repetition in those designs. What's going on with the dots and bars, you wonder?*

Can you figure out what purpose these symbols serve? See if you can crack the code.

Here are some of the patterns you find. Write the number of dots which appear below.

What is the highest number of dots which you find? _____

Does it matter if they are horizontal or vertical? _____

Do you have any theories as to what these dots might represent? _____

INTRODUCTION FIGURE 2.

You also find bars carved on the stone. Sometimes they are alone. Sometimes they are with dots.

Write the number of bars. Write the number of dots.

Dots _____
Bars _____

Dots _____
Bars _____

Dots _____
Bars _____

Dots _____
Bars _____

Dots _____
Bars _____

Dots _____
Bars _____

Dots _____
Bars _____

Dots _____
Bars _____

Dots _____
Bars _____

What is the largest number of bars that you found? _____ What is the largest number of dots? _____ Is it the same as earlier? _____

Do the dots or bars have to be the same size? _____ Does it matter if they are horizontal or vertical? _____

Exploring about the ruins, you notice more dot and bar combinations than here. For example, you find a stone with a "one bar and two dots" combination carved on it. Later, a "one bar and three dots" combination crops up. Is a pattern emerging, you wonder? But you never find a greater combination of dots or bars than you've already found.

Do you have any theories on what the dots and bars represent? Have your theories changed between the first counting of dots and this counting of bars?

INTRODUCTION FIGURE 3.

Often, the dots and bars appear in clusters, stacked on top of each other. (Lines have been put around each set to mark them off.)

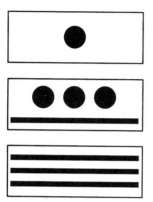

Mysteriously, a new symbol appears in some of the clusters, but never when dots or bars stand alone. It looks sort of like a shell.

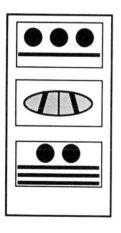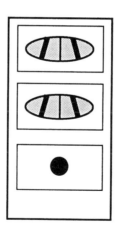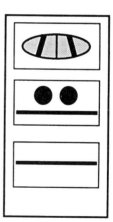

How many "shells" appear at a time? _____ Do they ever appear more than once as dots and bars do? _____ Does the shell ever appear at the bottom of the stack? _____

Do you have a theory what the shell might represent?

Do you have a theory why these symbols are stacked atop one another?

professional archaeologists have pored over and using the same tools of observation, inference, and discussion that had once cracked the Mayan codes.

Next we walked to see the casts of Copán stelae in the Peabody Museum exhibits. I asked everyone to examine them closely and then tell me what they could about the significance of numbers in Mayan society. Several people instantly noticed that numbers were ubiquitous in the Mayan texts. In an inscription that had twelve identifiable clusters of Mayan glyphs, seven of them contained numbers. Even in the longer inscriptions, Mayan numbers were more prevalent than any other symbol. Not fifteen minutes into our tour, the hall was buzzing with hypotheses about what the numbers could be recording. Soon came the conclusion that only time or money would warrant such meticulous accounting.

As the winter sky grew dark outside, we continued to talk and formulate questions. Led by those questions, we discussed how archaeologists like myself journey from such ample, but still very fragmentary, data to a portrait of a culture that we can only know through clues. Building on our work with the number system, I explained how decades of research on the Maya drew upon the same data to portray the Maya as peaceful counters of the days and months: a society ruled by calendar priests who were devoted to nothing more than the humble recording of time's infinite passage. However, as research has continued, this interpretation has proven less than accurate. New and different lines of data—in particular, many inscriptions dealing with the dates of battles and other acts of war—have caused a reevaluation of the pacifist time watcher hypothesis. In this way, even as we entered our research on the Maya together, we were able to touch on the very large questions of interpretation, new evidence, and the evolving nature of understanding another culture.

Building Up a Fund of Information

There is no avoiding it: in order to understand another culture framed in its own terms, you have to build up a fund of information. The unwaivable entrance fee consists of a real knowledge of climate, geography, ecology, history, language, art, economics, and symbol systems—all of which are keys to understanding. Here, too, the Mayan number system makes the point elegantly. Although it is possible to crack the Mayan numerical code within hours, understanding what it says about Mayan civilization is quite another matter.

In order to drive home my point, I asked the teachers for their patience as I showed them an enormous diagram of one of the Mayan calendars. Carefully I explained how the Maya conceived of time and the inner workings of their world as an infinite series of cycles: cycles of weather, agriculture, warfare, ritual, and the motions of the planetary bodies. I explained how the Maya kept accurate records of these and many other cycles through the use of their numerical system. With this background knowledge, and the luminous image of the vast carved calendar, teachers quickly gained access to the key to the cycles that are the very foundation of the Mayan worldview.

We went on to discuss how the most important cycles for the ancient Maya were recorded in a series of three calendars: a solar calendar, a ritual calendar, and a count of days. The solar calendar consists of 365 days divided into eighteen months of twenty days each and a nineteenth month of the five remaining days. The calendar, like ours, is based roughly on the amount of time it takes the earth to make one complete revolution around the sun. From the Mayan perspective, the calendar counts the days between the repetition of the sun's extreme positions in the sky. The solar calendar contains a total of nineteen month signs. The teachers deciphered this for themselves, given their knowledge of the numbering system.

I explained the rudiments of the Mayan ritual calendar, which is very hard to decipher. It is based on a cycle of twenty day names, and has thirteen cycles in all. This magic number of 260 days is not so much mathematical, as a biological pattern. This is the approximate period of human gestation, which is one of the prominent theories on its origin. This Mayan "long-count," as it is generally called, made possible a linear count of all the days since the beginning of time. For the ancient Maya this count forms a sort of grand temporal odometer counting off cycles of days, 20 days, 360 days,

20 × 360 days, 400 × 360 days. As in our culture, when the larger periods change, as with the coming millennium, it is cause for great celebration and a certain amount of reservation and expectation. As evidence from actual sites reveals, the Maya erected monuments on these special days at the ends of cycles. Although they erected more monuments at the end of large cycles, no cycle was too small to be commemorated, and markers of the passage of 20-day periods are common. Integral to the Mayan conception of time as cyclical was the notion that history would repeat itself. Thus, by keeping an accurate record of the past, one could likewise predict the future, as Mayan Jaguar Priests hoped to do.

At this point, I showed excerpts from an animated film version of the *Popol Vuh*, or *Book of Counsel*,[1] which details the Quiche Maya story of creation and served as a guide to a proper Mayan life. I promised not only that the film was beautiful, but that if participants would observe closely, this Mayan creation story would refine a number of the hypotheses we had formed through the analysis of Mayan numerical and calendrical systems. The film bombarded teachers with ancient images from classic Maya pottery depicting the players and the plots of the pre-Columbian epic. As the film ended, I asked, "So now what do you know about the Maya?" There was a flurry of observations:

"The Maya believed in multiple creations."
"They were by no means the first beings the gods created, and they wouldn't be the last."
"The Maya believed they were currently residing in the fourth creation. The three that preceded it had been unsatisfactory to the gods and were justly destroyed. None of the first three creations were able to worship the gods properly. Only the Maya, the people made from corn and blood, were able to please their creators."
"But that depended on them worshipping the gods carefully. They knew that this cycle of creation and destruction would not end with them. So their recording of the world's cycles was not only a count of time gone by but also a countdown of the time they had left in the current creation."

Together we returned to reading the *Popol Vuh*. This time around, I asked teachers to pick out whatever clues they could find about Mayan geography and cosmology. As they reviewed the images and described what they saw, we all became aware of how important successive levels appeared to be, as in the terraced landscapes and in the steeply stepped pyramids. Piecing together our observations—much as the larger community of archaeologists, all working on different aspects of current finds, does—along with the other texts, we came to the conclusion that the Maya conceived of a universe of three levels: the underworld, the middle world, and the heavens. I added what I knew from other sources: for the Maya, these levels were not entirely separated, and portals between them existed in both the natural and artificial landscapes. I asked, "Where would you find these kinds of portals to the underworld? To the heavens?" Drawing on images from the film of the *Popol Vuh*, teachers surmised that for the Maya, the underworld was a frightening place ruled by the Nine Lords of Death, which could be entered through the mouths of caves or the ballcourt. The heavens, where the deities and particularly revered ancestors resided, could be reached from mountain tops. In this cosmology, caves of the kind found at the top of mountains would be the critical junction of all three worlds:

"And what do you imagine would happen in such places?"
"Rituals."
"The homes of priests."
"Sacrifice and prayer."

At that moment, I asked "my students" to step back and think about how far we had built up our understanding of the Maya during the course of a single day. In those hours, we had journeyed from a single dot to a number system, through the cycles of the three calendars, and toward at least a beginning vision of the human lives and desires that could lie behind these visible artifacts. By carefully examining the *Popol Vuh*, we had come to see the Maya as a highly spiritual people. They conceived a universe that was alive at many levels. We expanded our rudimentary knowledge of numbers and the calendar to include a conception of

Mayan cyclical history and the geography of their sacred landscape. In reflection, we talked together about the importance of ample resources in creating a rich field of information. We agreed that at least part of our sense of accomplishment was the exhilaration of knowing so much more than we had at 9:00 that same morning. Now it was time to step even further back and look carefully at the process of turning information into evidence.

Digging Deep: The Art of Turning Information into Evidence

With these refined visions of Mayan ideology in hand, we were ready to dig deep into an ancient Mayan city. I told the teachers that they were archaeologists with the assignment of describing the functions of particular structures or groups of structures for which only fragments remained. We dimmed the lights and turned on the projector. Almost an entire wall filled with images of various Mayan structures nearly buried in the encroaching vegetation. I was ruthless, telling them, "No claims without being explicit," and "You have to defend your hypotheses on material, historical, or anthropological grounds."

Instantly, teachers identified the first structure as a temple. But that wasn't enough. I urged them to describe the process they went through, possibly unknowingly, to arrive at their conclusion.

"Well, it's really tall."

"Yes, the Maya constructed artificial mountains in the middle of their cities, with the doorway at the top representing a cave."

I showed them another slide. This one was from the ancient city of Copán, Honduras. One of the structures was even labeled with the Mayan hieroglyph for mountain, with the doorway surrounded by the teeth of the cave's mouth. The teachers were right. The higher the artificial mountain, the closer it was to the heavens, and thus, height did help to indicate function.

I asked, "Do you have other reasons?"

"The space at the top isn't very big, if I had the money to build such a large building, I'd want a bigger place to live in at the top;

also I wouldn't want to climb all those stairs. Maybe if someone could carry me . . ." answered one student.

I pushed, "If you are right, what would you expect to find as artifacts?"

We looked at slides of the interior.

"There is no sleeping bench inside. It's not likely to be living quarters," a student observed

"And I don't see any household debris. No bones or cloth," another added.

"Look at those large stone braziers. Could they be used for incense? For burning sacrifices?" still another student said.

I pointed to the carved stone lintel above the door.

"It looks like a figure, maybe a man, in a very elaborate costume, maybe burning incense," said a student.

"Are those what? Figures? Rising out of the smoke?" I said, urging them to look still more closely

We had dug deep into the layers of architectural evidence. We had built our hypothesis up gradually, slowly turning an initial hunch into a carefully researched conclusion. We went on to explore other structures. Surveying the whole site, the students picked out what they thought was a palace based on the extent of its living space.

"Now there's a place I wouldn't mind living, big, fancy, nice . . ."

"So what kind of evidence would prove or disprove that?" I asked

Observations poured out—each of them careful.

"Look, there are larger than usual rooms with sleeping benches."

"Big open courtyards."

"That looks like it could be a garbage dump with animal bones and pottery. So eating had to go on."

"Have a look at the building materials."

"It looks like cut stone. Most of the other houses we've seen were cobbles, or even mud and thatch."

"The stone is full of carving and hieroglyphic texts."

Again, teachers were right on. Mayan palace compounds are often a conglomeration of many living quarters for nobles, their extended families, servants, and retainers. These palaces are generally constructed of cut stone and are artistically elaborate, though some of the associated structures—servants' quarters, for example—may be less so. They may also include rooms designed for public audiences and still others for private ceremonies. There is very little domestic refuse associated with the nicest structures, as it was undoubtedly dumped elsewhere, generally behind the small, less elaborate structures in the compound. The quality of the refuse, when found, is generally high. Brightly decorated fine ceramic wares and animal bones indicate disposable wealth and a well-balanced diet. Professional archaeologists might have used technical terms, or tried their hand at data, or compared this site to others they had seen—but they would have done no better at the most basic work of digging for evidence to support their hypotheses.

Next, we compared the relative frequencies of the different structures. We looked at palace and elite residential compounds as compared to the number of shabbily constructed, presumably nonelite households. We compared the percentage of ceremonial architecture to domestic architecture and other classes of public and private spaces, such as ballcourts and workshops. From these comparisons we began to draw up a picture of the social structure of Mayan society. We had arrived at that critical point where it is possible to put people, daily lives, and possibly even motives and beliefs back into the picture.

Teachers were swift and clear in their observations:

"Most of the structures are for common people."
"The ceremonial architecture is all clustered in the center of the site."
"The houses for the elite and the palaces are located right nearby."
"The center of town is very elaborate artistically, especially compared to the suburbs. See, statues, sculptures on the faces of buildings, even painting.
"So . . . there must have been like full-time artists and stone carvers working for the ruling classes."

At that point, a flurry of questions broke out.

"So what else does that tell us?"

"So, did they have money?"

"Has anybody ever found contracts, I mean, were the artists slaves, or freemen?"

"Well, what kind of evidence would you need to find out?"

"I want something with more connections in it, something that will show me a scene. Are there Maya paintings that are like that . . . less stylized than glyphs or carvings?"

My questioner was on the money. One of the most important classes of data for exploring other cultures is art. Unfortunately, the sand in the seminar's hourglass had run out. If we'd had the extra hours, we would have continued digging in one of the great Mayan treasures, the Murals of Bonampak. There, in the magnificent scenes from the life of an archetypal Maya king, we would have dug even deeper into the spiritual life of the Maya. In so doing, we would have had the chance to rework the usual view of the Maya as savagely consumed by blood-letting and human sacrifice. We could have seen how their practices may have been tied to their view of themselves as "the people of corn and blood," whose survival depended on their penitent willingness to pay back the blood the gods had used to bring them to life.

We would have also looked at slides of contemporary Mayans. In general, when people think about the Maya, they think about abandoned cities in the rain forests of Guatemala, Mexico, and Belize. Most people outside Central America fail to realize that large and vibrant populations of Maya still exist in all three of those countries. That a modern Mayan culture exists today is part of an important lesson in thoughtful cultural exploration. When we deal with the question of what happened to the ancient Mayan cities, it is important not to imply that the Maya vanished. When we discuss the abandonment of those cities at the end of the ninth century, we are really discussing the decision of large numbers of people to change their way of life. It does not represent a fall from grace or the abrupt collapse of a civilization, as is often suggested. Millions of Mayans continue to plant corn and weave cloth and perform rituals in much the same way as they have for millennia. As such, modern Mayan society represents a multilayered weaving of ideas and practices that have been amassed over time. Traditional lifeways for the modern Maya are not passive behavioral remnants of times past, but active, conscious efforts to retain cultural/societal traits and practices in the face of external and internal impetuses for change.

As much as I wanted to conduct a tour of the murals and modern Mayan villages, perhaps it was not all bad that we failed to make the race to the finish. First of all, in pausing for discussion along the way, we lived out important lessons about depth rather than breadth of coverage. But more than that, having to stop short reminded us that archaeological data yield at best only a partial picture of human behavior. There will always be aspects of any culture for which there is no record or that we are unable to understand. Even though humans encode their material remains with meaning, this meaning can decay, or be vague or easily misunderstood.

Although it is the partial nature of archaeological knowledge that leads to misinterpretations as outlandish as aliens building the pyramids in Egypt, it is that same partial nature that makes archaeology an important lesson in thoughtful humanity. As I mentioned earlier, the greatest danger in teaching about other cultures is that, unintentionally, you may convey the notion that the people you are studying are not only different from you but that there is something unappealing or outright wrong about those differences. Every culture is different, and every culture possesses some traditions that others will find odd or even offensive. That the Maya practiced human sacrifice is a fact. But portraying them as bloodthirsty savages is unjust, and makes no effort to understand the underlying reasons that human sacrifice was integral to their way of life and view of the universe. Teaching archaeology as a series of amazing discoveries and persistent mysteries utilizes the subject's mass appeal but ignores its best qualities. Likewise, oversimplifying a culture for the sake of easy presentation and making it seem too much like ours are other hazards in teaching cultural exploration.

The archaeological methodology that we worked out in the curriculum seminars can help to avoid these pitfalls. It relies only on inquisitive problem solving and a humble mind. It provides students and teachers alike with the opportunity to participate in the ongoing act of discovery while encouraging respect for and understanding of other ways of life and other ways of thinking. The payoffs are simple.

In the modern world we are often faced with the illusion that there is precious little left to discover. We know where all the continents and oceans are. We've sent men to the moon and spacecraft hurtling out of the solar system. In reality, there are many realms of discovery still open to us: the oceans, space, the atom, and the human body—and all of the worlds that the archaeologist's work of digging deep can open up for the mind and the imagination.

Notes

1. *Popul Vuh: The Creation Myth of the Maya,* produced by Patricia Amlin, distributed by the University of California Extension Media Center, 2176 Shattuck Ave., Berkeley, CA 94704.

Prologue to Chapter 1
The Eagle and the Tortoise:
A Colleague's Tale

Nick Bartel

For three years, Marg Costello and I have worked together as social studies/language arts teachers for seventh graders at Horace
Mann Middle School in San Francisco. Together we have struggled
to clear a path through the jungles of our world history and cultures curricula—attempting to track down a way to organize and
teach large ideas and important attitudes to our students.

I am still impressed by the process by which Marg organizes a
unit. She does it intuitively, with great enthusiasm and energy,
soaring like an eagle into uncharted curricular skies, scanning for
connections that come clear to her only from above. I am more like
the tortoise in the Mayan legends: slower, ever in search of a road
map. I trudge along until I see how Marg has done it. I suspect
many of us teachers are linear thinkers who appreciate a map.
Give us a clear set of steps, and then we can practice, invent, and
internalize.

Marg's chapter provides us with the right kind of map. While it
is full of riches to be uncovered and studied, it also offers a very
clear image for thinking about how to integrate literature, history,
and geography, as well as current events and learning rooted in
community service. As I edited this chapter with her, that image
came into sharp focus. The unity of Marg's work is most like the
great Aztec calendar stone. At the very center is the culture to be
studied; it could be the Maya of Central America or the kingdoms
of West Africa. But this culture is never isolated or seen as an end in
itself; it becomes a canvas upon which universal themes of human

experience, current events, and the urgent questions of students' own developing lives can be explored. Like rays of the sun, radials stream out from the culture's center. One ray is history, with its stories to tell and wisdom to share with young adolescents. Another is literature, which makes it possible for students to see themselves reflected in the writing and images of others. The ray of current events demonstrates how well the lessons of history have been learned and applied by others. The ray of community work allows students to apply their understandings of the past and the present to their own neighborhoods, as well as to other parts of the world. A final and too often neglected ray is personal inquiry and growth—what Marg has come to believe is the source of resiliency.

"But wait," you might say, "we do this kind of integration all the time. What is so new about it?" Through working on this chapter, choosing words, finding examples, and thinking about what to highlight and what to omit, I think I have at least one answer to this question. It goes back to the "unity" that I mentioned earlier. It is not enough for the rays—the geography, the art, the literature—to be present. The radials have to illuminate, not just attach.

Take literature. We have learned that it is not enough simply to link a piece of young adolescent fiction to a particular culture. The potential danger of this is a thin or unrewarding connection. We want great pieces of literature, not convenient ones. Sometimes we are lucky and can turn to accessible works, such as folk tales, songs, or prayers. But often the great literature we want is simply too difficult and inaccessible for young readers. Determined, we have taken the liberty of excerpting what we can use, the first 130 pages of Alex Haley's *Roots*,[1] for instance. We have even turned to rewriting in order to guarantee that every student—bilingual and special education included—can read at least a version of the *Aeneid* when studying Rome, or *Sundiata: The Epic of the Lion King*[2] when studying the legendary founder of West African medieval kingdoms.

We need the very best literature from a culture. Only in that literature—and not in historical fiction—can we find the images, the events, and the ways of thinking that shaped peoples' lives in a particular time and place. Great literature has long-standing power because it speaks to universal human issues young people are faced with: their search for heroes, for instance, or their desire to understand the process of coming of age. We draw regularly on mythological heroes to alert students to the individuals in their community who have made moral and spiritual decisions and who influence others wisely. Since novels and tales occur in compressed time—showing characters facing, negotiating, and surviving crises in the time it takes to read thirty or a hundred pages—the characters' strategies and resiliency stand out boldly.

We are constantly moving back and forth between literature and life. For example, we often ask our students to reflect on their own resources by viewing themselves as characters and tracing their lifelines with the rites of passage typical of the culture from which they are descended. We also ask them to interview a parent or elder as a way of tying the past to the present, moving from history to the students' own expanding identities. If we speak to these issues, we can study any period, from anywhere in the world, and no one asks, "Why do we have to learn this?"

As teachers we have come to count equally on the arts and cultural practices of the civilizations we study. We try to put into students' hands the same materials (or nearly so) used by the culture they are studying: the small chips of color that make up Byzantine mosaics, mud paintings and adinkra prints of West Africa, Chinese brush paintings, and block printing such as those produced for centuries in Japan. Once students have tried to create meaning with those same materials, they have a deeper respect for what masters elsewhere have made. We open up the worlds of performance as well: Chinese opera, Japanese Kabuki puppets, even Shakespeare. But along with these "high" arts, we insist on introducing the everyday face of a culture. We bring games of the place and period to our students, such as African mancala, medieval and Chinese chess, and Japanese Goh. And, thanks to Crock-Pots and electric woks, we cook. Again, someone might ask, "So what is new here?" The answer, I believe, is in the newspaper on the table and the dishes in the sink. We don't simply look at reproductions of Japanese wood block prints; we make them, cutting tools and all. We cook ground-nut stew. Carving and stirring slowly produce their own forms of knowledge and respect.

It is perhaps the other radials, the current events and the community service, that will strike people as innovations. Students usually view history as being shut off from the present. Our approach is to tie the past to the present with current events. In this endeavor, newspapers and magazines have always been our allies; more recently, the Internet has become a powerful partner. For example, when we initially developed our study of Rome and Spartacus's slave revolt, we augmented that discussion by reading *Roots*. From there we built a natural bridge to modern-day coverage of human rights. We then discussed child labor as it is currently practiced in the growing fields of California.

Once a week, Marg's students are required to read the daily paper or another periodical and bring in an article that relates to the culture that they are studying. As Marg taught her unit on the Maya, students brought in a steady stream of articles from their morning papers: on the continuing importance of the rain forests for biodiversity; issues of Mayan rights in contemporary politics; the debate over the repatriation of Mayan artifacts bought by collectors and museums in the United States; and the discovery of the body of the "Inca Ice Maiden," a young adolescent girl's skeleton recently discovered and thought to hold clues to that ancient civilization. We have also reached out to organizations such as IDEX (International Development Exchange), the Peace Corps, UNICEF, or the Red Cross. For instance, when Marg was studying the Maya, the IDEX people visited the school to talk about the issues facing the modern Maya. This emphasized the fact that the Maya are still very much a living people, struggling to adapt their culture to a changing environment.

To this, we have tried to add the radial of community service. Marg's students not only studied the issues of child labor in California's fields, they also wrote to the White House and to two state senators to express their concern that individuals their own age were essentially enslaved, picking vegetables and fruit for our tables. When the students received the replies to their letters, they were impressed by the glossy photographs from Washington. They were much more taken with the White House letter than the reply from one of their state senators. But Marg got them to stop and think. She asked them to compare the letters in order to discover which one really replied to their questions. Students were surprised to find that their senator's letter—although it contained no autographed photos—actually answered their specific questions in detail. These connections signal to students that there are some large human issues on which they can take action.

As middle school teachers, perhaps our greatest challenge—whether we are eagles or tortoises—is to engage our students in the great lessons of history and literature, showing how cultures and individuals grow and change, react to their environments, and through trial and error arrive at a period of stability—perhaps even attaining greatness. Marg and I have come to believe that we can't afford to stop at appreciation. For us, the radials of current events and community service are essential. We teach best when we show our students the reverberations between the central issues in their own lives and what history and literature have to offer. They can see then that the situations that engulf or threaten them have been played out in, or can be illuminated by, lives lived in other times and places.

Marg speaks of the "You are here" signpost in the middle of the jungle in Central America. It's an apt marker for us all. Through the integrated teaching that Marg lays, students can find a place for themselves in the "here" that we all share.

Notes

1. A. Haley. 1976. *Roots*. New York: Doubleday.
2. R. Berton. 1970. *Sundiata: The Epic of the Lion King*, retold. Illustrated by Gregorio Prestopino. New York: T. Y. Crowell Co.

You Are Here

*A Cultural Exploration of the Maya and
Seventh Graders*

Marg Costello

Magic, mystery, Mayas . . . my body is still drenched from the intense humidity of the rain forest surrounding Tikal . . . my head is still reeling from the ascent to the tops of pyramids and temples that emerge like skyscrapers above the forest canopy in Palenque . . . my imagination is teased and tortured by the stellar glyphs of Copán and her majestic hieroglyphic stairway made from 2,500 blocks of stone, each with a carved hieroglyph still to be understood . . . my dreams are haunted by the shadows of the moonlit night jungle, and the cacophony of insect sounds and screeches of howler monkeys pounding the dark silence. These incredible builders of civilization, the Maya, surround and astound me as my travel partner and I gaze together at the plethora of constellations in the summer sky against an illuminated backdrop of lightning in the Sierra Madre and ask, "Why did the Maya's ancestors leave these places?" Can the voices of these still surviving and adapting people have any influence upon or relevance to my students' lives? When I return to teaching, months and miles from now, can their centuries-long endurance create the foundation for an evolving discussion with my students about their own resources and their capacity for resilience, that is, why seventh graders and cultures like that of the Maya make it, in spite of great odds?

I remembered these thoughts upon returning to San Francisco after a summer of adventure in the Yucatán of Mexico and the rain forests and ruins of Guatemala and Honduras. But my even bigger concern was, how do I bring the "then and here" to the "here and now"? How can my students appreciate and value the Central American cultures that are so much a part of the culture of our city's schools? How could my students—whether they are Latino or Chinese—use their awareness of another culture as the cornerstone of becoming an active and concerned citizen? What are the chances that what we discuss when we study the Maya could translate into protesting anti-immigration policies like Proposition 187 or writing letters in opposition to the University of California Regents' policy against affirmative action in their admissions?

Participation in the PACE project and the curriculum seminar in cultural explorations was my springboard and impetus for visiting Central America. The discussions with other teachers challenged me to begin my curricular unit by first thinking about the bigger questions that would thread throughout my year-long instruction, such as "What are the similar patterns, rhythms, symbols, and questions in cultures ancient, modern, and emerging? What are the connections between humans, nature, and their spiritual inner and outer worlds? Why is the process of archaeology always unfinished? What difference does it make to hypothesize about a culture and dig for supporting evidence?"

I wanted to engage students in the process of inquiry. I want them questioning, thinking, and reflecting. These are life-long habits of mind that will empower them. I wanted them to see their connectedness to these ancient, yet living, people and to generate probing, but respectful, questions as the best archaeologists do. I wanted them to make hypotheses, examine artifacts, look for evidence, listen to the evidence of the "experts" and their peers, and then revisit and review their hypotheses about what really happened to the Mayan cities of the classic period. I wanted them to integrate their findings through language arts in the construction of their own Mayan myths and weave together the seamless Mayan reality of the inner and outer worlds. Furthermore, I wanted to begin the complex task of introducing both an awareness of the modern world and service learning as bridges between the past, the present, and themselves.

Enter Here

In the seminar, we talked about enriching the subject of world history with cultural exploration, asking students to take on the role of archaeologists. We also discussed how much this depended on finding one or more "entry points": immediate cross-sections of a given civilization that tantalize students into making predictions about what is to come.

So I knew I was hunting for an entry point that would introduce my students to a people still as vibrant and alive as the colors of their weaving, yet whose ancient ruins remain as shrouded in mystery as their volcanoes are in clouds. It was in the midst of the Peten rain forest, deep in the heart of Guatemala, that I stumbled upon it. We came upon a Tikal signpost planted squarely in the moist soil of the Guatemalan jungle, currently crisscrossed by an army of leaf-cutter ants. A white circle was painted in its center with the English words "You are here" scrawled boldly across it. Although we all chuckled, I may have been the most delighted. No question: the best entry point would be August 28, 1996, the first day that bright-eyed, eager, enthusiastic, hormonally challenged seventh graders would flood into the room where I, very recently returned from the land of the Mayan stairmasters, would be waiting.

I would be standing on the first floor of Horace Mann Academic Middle School, located in the heart of San Francisco. We serve 620 students in grades six, seven, and eight. We are a culturally rich and diverse student body and staff. Approximately 39 percent of the student body are Latino, 17 percent European American, 8 percent African American, 7 percent Filipino, 12 percent Chinese and 13 percent of mixed ancestry. They would also be pouring into the first day of our Awareness Month, which opens each year. In recognition of our diversity, we inaugurate our year with activities, assemblies, and contests that explore issues of racism, sexism, ageism, homophobia, and the treatment of the physically challenged. We investigate stereotypes and intolerance in our school, community, city, or global village. After a month of work toward solutions, we end with a culminating assembly by staff, rife with comedy, on how to treat and appreciate one another's diversity. Awareness Month would be my first point of entry in our cultural exploration of the Maya.

August 28th came, and I met the fifty seventh graders who would make up my morning and afternoon "core" classes. (Core refers to the language arts/social studies class that each seventh-grader takes.) Our first week was a time to teach the cooperative social skills that we would all need to work successfully together. Student teams created placards that described what would be important to their success and posted them throughout the class-room:

No put-downs or teasing
No racism
Think positive and use positive words
Respect everything and everyone
Never say "I can't"
Active listening
Always be prepared

We were, in effect, beginning to create a distinctive classroom culture. We created a keen sense that when you enter Room 152, "You are *here.*"

Working from that shared "here," we began to explore what each student brought to Room 152 from his or her home culture. For homework, each student listed the ten to twenty most important things (beliefs, events, people) in his or her life. As an investment in learning to infer culture from artifacts, I asked them to bring objects from home that represented or symbolized these important values, customs, and relationships. The next day students brought in pictures of their little brothers and sisters or pit bulls (many similar characteristics!), leaves from trees, traditional clothes from the Philippines, and the remote controls to their TV sets. Some students simply named things like warmth and love. To plant the idea that our thoughts and insights are never complete, I gave them a chance to amend their lists, based on all that they had seen and heard from one another.

We took a step from personal to larger cultures when I asked my students to make a list of ten to twenty things that are important to our shared culture and bring artifacts to class that represent those values. Students wrote their items on a large sheet of butcher paper in the front of the room as they reported to the class. Once every child had recorded his or her contribution, I again asked, "What things are left out?" Then I pushed. I asked, "How can thinking about what is important to us help us better understand the Maya?" I half-expected a pause, or worse yet, silence. Instead, this is what I heard:

> We could think what was important to the Mayas and then piece little ideas at a time until we have a picture in our minds of what they did and what was really important to them. We can also try to picture them and what they did to get an idea of how life was in Mayan civilization. We also can picture ourselves and think what we would have done and might better understand how the Maya lived.
>
> —*Christopher Rivera*

> If we think about what is important to us, it can probably help us because probably the people we are influenced by have Mayan blood in them so we can kinda relate to them. It also helps because if I know how I feel and how I think, I can understand them since they too are people. They had beliefs and civilization like we do. It can show us how different we are from the Mayans. They valued the same things we do such as food and clothing.
>
> —*April Damian*

Reading these responses made it clear to me that these students were starting to see a personal connection to the Maya.

As a culminating piece, I shared a set of remarkable poems with my students. The poems were written as part of a project, "Redescubiendo America," by Michelle Banks and Enrique Aviles. In these ethnoautobiographical poems, students used a frame to begin:

> They ask me to write down
> my race
> and I think
> very seriously
>
> and consider
> writing down the truth
> and have my answer read. . . .

That frame sparked candid and often beautiful writing about the cultures that students knew coursed through them. This poem, from our class, won first place for seventh grade in the schoolwide poetry contest:

> They ask me to write down
> my race
> and I think
> very seriously
>
> and consider
> writing down the truth
> and have my answer read
>
> I have an old lady
> who I call "Lola"
> she cooks
> gardens
> cleans
> inside this body
>
> I have a mom
> she helps me become
> what I want to be
> a doctor
> successful
> educated
> religious
> inside this body
>
> I think about
> The Witches

Pinocchio
The Giving Tree
Beauty and the Beast
and how they all had happy endings
wishing my life
would turn out the same
inside this body

They ask me to write down
my race

and I think
and think
very seriously

and consider
writing down the truth
and have my answer read

I think about
my ancestors
who came before me
who struggled
who fought
so I would be given
a fair chance
inside this body

I think of the native
dances
songs
fashions
of my country
how they make me proud
inside this body

But I stop
and simply
write down
FILIPINO

The poems, collages the students made to represent themselves, and photos I took of them at work made a mural that surrounded us. At last, we had a physical "here and now" that was uniquely our own. We were ready to find and know the "here" that had been and remains Mayan culture.

Becoming Archaeologists

These students weren't novices. They had survived studying all of the ancient world in sixth grade. They knew how to read, to take notes, and to ask questions about what puzzled them. But that left them good students, not yet archaeologists. They needed two more skills in their kit: sharp-eyed observation and a severe case of curiosity.

Immediately, I distributed my newly formed collection of artifacts from the Mayan world. I handed out arrows, ceremonial knives, stelas, statues, pictures, coins, cloth, stories, and weavings to each student team. Not a word of explanation. I simply asked them to sketch their items so carefully that they could discover what the Maya valued. By way of beginning a discussion of evidence, I told them to be ready to give three supporting reasons for each claim that they made.

Kelly Mostert, examining a small Mayan ceramic sculpture, wrote underneath her sketch:

> I think the Maya value nature (their plants and agriculture) because the man or god or whatever is holding a plant in a pot. I think they value decorations on themselves because he looks like he is performing a ceremony and he is decorated weird (for me, not weird for him).

Cynthia Mena sketched a ceremonial sacrificial knife with a winding serpent on the handle and noted that it symbolized how tough the Maya could be and that they worshipped their animals. Both of these examples illustrate the beginning of building hypotheses.

Using photos of students examining their objects, I created a bulletin board captioned "Who They Are" for Back-to-School

Night. Watching that evening, I was amazed to see students draw their family members over to the table of artifacts, explaining their significance. More than once, I heard students ask their families if they were of Mayan ancestry. Several families proudly explained their links to these ancient peoples. One student of mixed ancestry, who does not know who her biological father is, told her foster mother that she now felt that part of her ancestry was Maya!

I knew that we had to begin to raise questions: no questions, no inquiry. So, based on their studies of the artifacts, I asked students to create a huge, butcher-paper sheet full of the questions they had when they first "met" their artifacts. I also asked them to list any new questions that had emerged from the class discussion. Students generated a flood of questions about the Maya.[1] Many of them focused on "cultural universals." How did they educate their kids, eat, marry, handle death, find recreation, or arm themselves for hunting? Other questions focused on what was unusual or intriguing: What about human sacrifice? Did it hurt when they pierced their penis? Did girls get pierced somewhere? How long did it take to carve those statues? Were they crazy or weird? Why were they so fascinated with the solar system? Did the Maya have any record of the earliest Maya that we haven't heard about? The seventh-grade mind never rests!

Generating these questions proved we had the goods to be budding archaeologists. Posted where we could all see them, the questions would also be our talismans. They would keep us safe, protecting us from blind lecturing and passive note taking as we entered the world of the Maya. In their honor, we agreed that every week we would answer more of the questions, add new information, or correct wrong statements. My students had their assignment as archaeologists clearly in mind.

But what exactly does an archaeologist do? I distributed a grid for them to complete while watching a National Geographic video on the Maya. I wanted them to notice and describe specific things Maya archaeologists did and are still doing among the hundreds of Mayan ruins in Central America. On it they had to record what an archaeologist sees, does, thinks, feels, and asks questions about.

Lucy Parada recorded that an archaeologist thinks about the

kinds of religions the Maya had, about where the tunnels led, that the artifacts they dig up are incredible works of art, that the culture is sophisticated, that every day they are learning more about the Maya and how they lived. She listed the following questions as being posed by archaeologists in the video:

> Who built this place? Why had the city been abandoned? What happened to the city? What kinds of food did they eat? Did they have more than one religion? What crafts did they do? How did the Maya think about death? What's inside the buildings? Who painted the pictures? What do they mean? Who were their enemies? When will the rain end?

Carrie Yu recorded that an archaeologist sees buildings, statues, stones, rocks, secret passages, doors, royal stuff, horoscopes, temples, books, colored buildings, blood stains, tombs, masks, birds, and scorpions. For her, an archaeologist

> searches, discovers; chops trees to get through; records; directs people; pieces things together; recovers; peels; uncovers; climbs; investigates caves, bushes, and city sites; and works with weavers.

She imagined that an archaeologist must feel

> excited, confounded, surprised, touched, love, amazement. "My God, let's get out of here," sad, lonely, wonderful, "I have to find out the truth," ambitious.

Students came away from the films with a strong visual picture, not only about what a Maya archaeologist does and feels, but of the Mayan ruins and the tremendous amount of interconnected guesswork that goes into interpreting archaeological evidence. In fact, students were learning that archaeologists are thinking, feeling men and women like us! . . . "You are here."

Perhaps remembering the weavings and the carved stone knives we examined earlier, a number of students had asked whether we had firsthand sources about Mayan life. This led to my second point of entry, the Aztec codices, about—what else?—puberty. Not only were we "here," but they were there too! I wanted to share a sample of one of the few remaining Maya codices. But, as is often true in the world of archaeology, the record is partial, destroyed, or, at the very least, hard to get at. After some comparison to what the students had learned about Egyptian glyphs last year, I explained that most of the Maya codices were destroyed by the Spanish and Catholic priests. Only four are known to still exist: one in Paris, the Peresianus Codex; the Dresden Codex, which explains the gods and astronomy; one in Madrid, Spain, that consists of horoscopes and almanacs to assist priests in their predictions and ceremonies; and one in New York. Together we speculated about why one culture might want to destroy another's books, and I asked if they knew of other times when this happened in history. I then explained that I was able to get a copy of two Aztec codices from *The Conquest of Mexico*.[2] I distributed a copy to each person, and asked them as a team to determine how it folded, in what order it was read, and how to interpret the meaning of side one. Like archaeologists in the real world, they were having to come to know a culture through its translations and descendants—with all the questions that raises.

After studying the codex, one student hypothesized that the illustrations and glyphs narrated this story:

> A child was born and given to a priest to raise. As the child grew, he had the power to talk to death but death is not always nice. The child then gave birth to a child and death told him to give the child to him. Later death asked for a sacrifice of the older child and to have his blood.
>
> —*Piccola Ellison*

Another student independently wrote:

> The black thing the guy is holding is a baby. The baby grows up to be a juggler and everyone watches his act. The guy who is bending on one knee is the juggler and he is older now as he watches his daughter have a baby. The juggler dies and the guy of the bony structure is the king of death and he carries the juggler off.
>
> —*James Valerio*

After much speculation and theorizing, I gave them a published archaeologist's answer:

> The witch goddess, with a serpent round her waist, is presenting a newborn child to the goddess of death. A bird (the child's soul) hovers above.
>
> A young man with a string of beads round his neck is standing on the head of the Earth monster. He is dying, perhaps from an epileptic fit, and the god and goddess of the star of death are easing him out of his mortal body.
>
> A mother sits in a maize field and sings a lullaby to her baby, but the god of death cuts down an ear of maize, which also looks like the body of the plumed serpent with its articulated spine. Behind the god the bird of ill omen is croaking as he nests in a cactus. This suggests that the baby will be mown down by death.
>
> A young priest or noble makes offerings—including a black hairless dog—to the god of death. He places on an anvil an object that looks like the symbol for "blossoming war." This was a strange concept suggesting that out of suffering and death something might flower. Here we see that the god is accepting the offering with pleasure. The young man looks happy and has transcended his pain.[3]

Immediately, my students asked the right question: "How did those archaeologists come to the conclusions they did?" I asked them if they had ever read the same book but interpreted the meaning differently, and so gave a different report, or wrote a different paper. They all had. Now we were doing the hard work of drawing inferences from the data we could get our hands on. We were also knee-deep in the even harder work of wrestling with what we would take as a "good" or "reasonable" explanation.

I told them I would give them a clue to the second side. It had something to do with how the Aztecs viewed puberty (a topic close to their hearts!). Away they went! As they worked, these new illustrations put my students in touch with the humanity of the Aztec people as individuals who experienced similar thoughts, feelings, and drives, and who didn't have an easy time growing up. At this point, I had established what would become an ongoing discussion of puberty and rites of passage that we would revisit throughout the year. This was also our first chance to touch on the theme of resiliency, or the ability to bounce back no matter what hand life has dealt you. It gave us a chance, as adult and adolescents, to talk about how they could draw on the protective strategies already present in their pubescent repertoire: their physical and psychological energy, health, and humor.

The "Here" of the Popul Vuh

Everyone has the questions: "Who are we?" "Where did we come from?" "How do you know?" Students were given these questions to answer for homework in their "Archaeological Journal" along with an assignment to interview an adult in their house for their thoughts. The next day in class, I held up a copy of the *Popul Vuh*,[4] which literally means "Collection of Written Leaves," and explained that these were the same questions all our ancestors in all cultures asked, and we still debate. The *Popul Vuh*, I explained, is thought to record Mayan answers to these very questions. We talked about the fact that the original version was done in pictures or glyphs, then translated by a Maya to a Spanish priest who then recorded it in written Spanish. Since many of my students are bilingual, we could talk about how translation can change the meaning, particularly when the translator highlights aspects of the story similar to his own experience or culture—for instance, viewing the *Popul Vuh* as the Maya Bible. We even discussed the implicit judgment that occurs when people refer to these stories as creation *myths*.

   As much as the *Popul Vuh* gave us an occasion to think about cultural values, it provided an opportunity—like many others throughout our exploration—to build the other face of resilience: knowledge. I insisted that my students know what the setting was, who the main characters were, and how the plot developed through the conflict, turning point, and resolution. That night, students drew a codex for the story of "The Twin Brothers." The codex had to be drawn in the order and style of a Mayan codex. That meant it had to be a plausible reflection of what they had seen in the Aztec codex, but adapted to use Mayan symbols like glyphs and numerals, values and practices, as well as the characteristic details and styling action of Mayan images such as flattened foreheads and a procession of figures in a complex scene. After all, someone who is going to become resilient has to be able to integrate understandings.

Some students gave back answers that reflected their religions or education, like "We came from monkeys . . ." or "God made us." Others struggled uncertainly with these questions, supported by the uncertainty of their parents.

Next, we watched an excellent animated version of the *Popul Vuh*[5] that artfully blended and merged character glyphs of the spiritual worlds with the earthly ones, giving students a better sense of the interconnected, seamless reality of the Maya. At the end of the video I posed a series of questions:

What were the similarities and differences between the written and animated versions of the *Popul Vuh*?
Which one do you think was closer to the "original" Mayan version? Why?

I also had the kids write essays. Roy's analysis showed how critically and thoughtfully students can interpret visual information:

I think the video of the Popul Vuh was more similar to the way the Maya would write their codex story. The printed story of the "Twin Brothers" seems so retold. The video of the Popul Vuh was more spiritual and more fantasy or more of the beliefs of the Mayans. The video involved all of the animals and it mentioned all the foods from the ground known to the Mayas. The printed story was told in English and the video had some Mayan words. Both stories were good but the Popul Vuh video was much better because it was about nature, and the printed story was more about a lesson that everyone should follow.

Enriching the Information

We were headed toward being able to think about what happened to the great classic Mayan cities. But I had no interest in inviting my students only to guess. Like any archaeologist, I wanted them to be as informed as possible. So we spent time reading and researching the Olmec civilization on which the Mayan culture was built, paying special attention to theories about what caused the fall of those cities. We also studied the geography of the region. We watched the Time-Life video *Blood of Kings* for more background information on the religious and spiritual life of the Maya. (Students were particularly intrigued by bloodletting rituals and, in particular, by the queen piercing her tongue and running a twined cord of thorns through it and the king piercing his foreskin!) We paused to study the Mayan number system and created an interlocking Mayan calendar, reflecting on what the existence of such technologies implied about Mayan civilization.

Edwin Ramos Jr. took this as an opportunity to think aloud about time, transcribing his thoughts. As a teacher I love reading this over because I can hear him consciously connecting what he is learning with his own previous knowledge and experience, just as an archaeologist does.

Time. Time is a wonderful thing if you know how to use it of course. Time has been used for centuries, even in Mayan times according to the evidence we have found, time is something you use for several events like to know when your birthday is and other important things. We keep track of it so that we know ahead of time when special events are coming: for example marriage, in order to know the date of your marriage, you have to keep track of time so that you won't forget and let it pass by. The way we measure time in the US is by twelve months a year.

When I found out the true way the Maya kept track of time, I said to myself they must have had a really good memory. Either that or they had a really easy system that was in everybody's nature when they were born, or something like that. As soon as I found out the true way that the Maya kept track of time I compared it and asked myself what similarities do we have by the way we keep track of time to the way the Maya keep track of time? The first one I thought of were the disks, when they move independently, that can be related to the way the arms on our clocks move independently and tell us the time. The second one that popped out of my head was the carvings or paintings . . . that can be related to the numbers that are painted on the clock. Another one that I thought of was the disk. Usually disks are round and the old-fashioned way of keeping track of time was on a round disk. What similarities can you think of besides the ones I mentioned?

The Final Project: What Became of the Mayan "Here"?

It was time for my armchair archaeologists to get their boots muddied in the mire of my Mayan artifacts, videos, and slides. (I didn't have the heart to tell them that I had also visited the other parts of the world we are going to study.) Each team was assigned an ancient Mayan center: Uxmal, Chichen Itza, Palenque, Tikal, or Copán. Students had to work out the potential reasons the Mayan civilizations collapsed at their particular location, building their hypotheses in the light of what other archaeologists have argued as to why Palenque, Tikal, and Copán came to an end.

Each student archaeological team was given an "excavation site," consisting of approximately forty slides with corresponding guidebook descriptions, maps, and site information; a video on their site, most of which included a discussion of Mayan beliefs and practices at that site; plus miscellaneous artifacts particular to that site. In addition, they were free to use whatever other sources they could lay their hands on: adults they knew, public libraries, and the Internet. I explained that the sites they were to investigate still had many areas unexcavated. They were to continue to build on the previous archaeological evidence to further their own theories as to why the

Mayans left that particular location. Additionally, they were to draw on existing information in their archaeological tool bag, i.e., the Mayan calendar and number systems, glyph information, historical information gleaned from their texts, geographic information, and insights gleaned from the Mayan literature we had read thus far, to assist in the construction of their own theory.

Specifically each archaeological team was to make a presentation which was dramatic, visual, or oral, educating an audience about their site and its demise. I shared these criteria for their project:

1. Provide the dates and known history (government, religion, social organization, trade patterns, housing, farming, art) of the civilization known to inhabit the site.
2. Highlight and describe unique archaeological features of the site and their purposes, e.g., the ballcourt and the games played there.
3. Present the archaeological team's theory as to why, when, and over what period of time this center was vacated and hypothesize as to where the inhabitants might have gone. In all cases provide supporting evidence.

To animate this process, students had to name their archaeological team and select a Mayan animal spirit and god to guide their dig. What I enjoyed most about the naming process is that it provided still another way for kids to bridge the inner and outer world of the Maya. Here is an email message that a group of students sent to their editors back at PACE:

The Weaved Stories   Chimpanzees   Khauk (God of Life)

We are studying the ancient Mayans of Copan. We chose the name Weaved Stories because the ancient Maya weaved their special life stories in their cloth. We chose our animal spirit because it resembled something we would like to remember about our group. They take care of themselves as well as their "team mates," they have high energy and are very high spirited. We would much like to think of those things when we think of the Weaved Stories. We chose our god because he is the god of life. We feel that that is a very important part so we thought maybe we could show our appreciation by remembering him to our group.

At the end of this process, we all sat back to catch our collective breath. In that moment, I asked my students if I was a failure as a teacher because I couldn't answer all the questions we had up on the wall. In fact, because of our archaeological adventure together, I now had even more questions. At first they had no answer, but when I returned to this question a month later, they were sure it was right to be full of questions.

Thinking About the Inner "Here" of the Maya

We still had to tell posterity "true stories" of the abandonment of these majestic cities. I also wanted a way to emphasize that each one of my students was responsible not just for accumulating but for being able to use the huge store of information we had built together. Toward this end, I asked each student to write a "myth" from a Mayan point of view, for which they would be evaluated on their individual ability to adopt the voice and stance of an inhabitant from their chosen site. From that point of view they were to:

- include 3–5 significant events that capture Mayan culture at that site
- explain why the site collapsed
- describe clues that a future archaeologist might use to figure out what happened to that civilization
- use at least 3–5 "show, not tell" words in each paragraph
- use at least 3 similes or metaphors in the myth
- have a clear beginning, middle, and end with a clever clincher
- use grammar, spelling, and sentence structure effectively to communicate your ideas
- create a full-page glyph or codex that supports the main message or theory in your myth as to why your people left
- incorporate at least two suggestions from your group's revision team
- incorporate two suggestions for improvement that came from your own self-reflection

The following is an excerpt from April Damian's myth as told by one of the great animal spirits, Itzamna, who walked the earth in the shape of a beautiful peacock. She explains the fall of Copán as Itzamna's revenge. In the opening pages she creates a highly detailed picture of the daily life of farmers, artisans, and priests. The climax of the story takes the form of a high-stakes game at the ceremonial ballcourt. It is a game of life and death in which Copán meets Quirigua in a battle for all the trade routes of the Mayan world.

> The time came. Copán vs. Quirigua. This was for all the trade routes. Not only did the lives of my people depend on this, but also my own. It began. The ball went up into the air. Quirigua hit the ball up into our side—Flapa gave it the hip—Quirigua bumped it with his head—it came so close to the hoop—Leon got it with his elbow—Quirigua blasted the ball straight towards the hoop with their chests. Everyone stopped what they were doing as they watched the ball move closer and closer into the hoop. It went through. The people of Copán and myself could feel the agony of defeat in our minds and our hearts. But then, the spirit of the peacock came to us and said, "Do not be afraid for the mighty Itzamna will bring all of you, both good and bad, into the heavens where you will live eternally." The peacock spirit left. As soon as it left, many of the people of Copán were transformed into doves. They looked at each other with awe as their feathers glistened in the warm, smiling sun. Their eyes sparkled and twinkled like shining stars in the peaceful sky. They all flew into the heavens, satisfied with what had happened to them.
>
> So it happened. Quirigua took power over all the trade routes, the city-state of Copán was vacated, and most of the people of Copán were all gathered around a table in the heavens enjoying themselves and the company of others. But ah! The story doesn't end their [sic]. You're probably wondering what happened to the Mayans that still live. "Where did they go?" you ask. Well, there were those who

chose not to fly up to the heavens. They instead migrated to other Mayan civilizations such as Piedras Negras. The lord of Piedras Negras thought that the people of Copán didn't deserve to have a special job. He then decided to make them all slaves. The slaves who once were given the opportunity to become doves in the heavens were now suffering in the hot, humid land of Piedras Negras. Their [sic], they and their children were to suffer eternally—FOREVER.

What's Left? The Resiliency of Using Understanding in the Service of Others

The Mayas are left! They didn't disappear from their homelands of Mexico, Belize, Guatemala, Honduras, or El Salvador but only abandoned over time their mausoleums to past glory. My students were only peripherally aware of this concept as we chiseled away at the magical mystery surrounding the Maya. It was time to make that point and to expand our work in history to contemporary social consciousness through the practice of service learning.

I invited a guest speaker from IDEX (International Development and Educational Exchange) to set the stage. She started with slides showing major industrial centers in the developing world and asked the students where they thought these pictures were taken. Most guessed the United States and were surprised to learn that they were taken in Central America, Africa, and Asia. The speaker helped my students connect with the learnings from Awareness Month and see that while we often stereotype people in our own country, our images of other countries in the world can also be too narrow or oversimplified. She probed the reasons that this can happen, bringing to the surface the role of government and the media in the portrayal of these cultures.

She then showed them slides of the Maya living today in Guatemala, telling the story of what has happened to them since the Spanish arrived in the 1500s. Included in her discussion was the role of the United States; companies such as United Fruit, Del Monte, and ultimately United Brands; as well as the last thirty-five years of civil war and the unearthing of massive grave sites of murdered Indians.

For homework that night, students had to read a newspaper, magazine, or Internet article on any news about the area, people, or culture of Central America or United States citizens or residents of Latino descent. Students had to be prepared to answer three questions: What did you learn? What picture in your mind did the article give you? What questions do you still have? This type of assignment is ongoing throughout the school year so that students can see the links between the past and the present, between cultures that we have studied, and the influence of each particular culture in our own country. This activity echoes our awareness discussions from the first months of school as we recognize the contributions of my students' ancestors from the Americas, Africa, China, Japan, the Middle East, and Europe, and explore the challenges each of these groups currently face in our country.

Our guest speaker from IDEX interacted with students as they reported, and then she presented to them a current dilemma facing a Mayan village high up in the Sierra Madre. The village was unable to eke out a living by subsistence farming and needed a source of income collectively for the village. Students were split into two groups and given all the data they needed to examine the village's economic resources.

I asked my students if there was anything we could do to help. I supplied them with a list of community projects for which the people of Guatemala have requested monetary assistance from IDEX. Each class carefully considered and debated various proposals before reaching a consensus. My morning class decided that low-cost housing was most important (as this is a key issue in their lives) and chose to fund a cooperative that provided a revolving fund loan to families in their village. My afternoon class felt that with the end of the civil war, violence against the Indians still needed to be watched, especially since they had already lost a great deal of good land. This group decided to fund a video project to monitor human rights violations in the mountains. Their funds would provide solar batteries to run the equipment. Each class determined what needed to be done to complete its project. The next day I gave them a paper with their decisions and organization. Away they went. We raised $160 for the housing project and $210 for the human rights project; both amounts were matched by an outside agency. In addition to all the language arts and social studies skills developed, I had to introduce many economic concepts, such as revolving loans and supply and demand, particularly when planning and assessing our fund-raising efforts.

After each group had reported, our speaker showed slides of the village and explained what the village actually decided to do. They had opted for the co-op. Cheers erupted from the team that had chosen to do the same. She went on to explain that the IDEX helped with the capital outlay of the sewing equipment and that the cooperative had been self-sustaining and profitable for the last two years as demands for Guatemalan cloth were high. But now, the cloth is no longer in demand, and the cooperative is operating at a loss and has to rethink the age-old problem of being pushed off the best land by banana plantations, wealthy land owners, or the government.

Final Thoughts

Time ran out. Another schoolwide activity from a science project our school is part of, Project 2061, disabled our smooth transition from the Maya to service learning. Still determined, my students selected a human rights project and worked out ways to raise funds for it. But I want to hang on to it. This type of service learning not only meets a community need identified by the Guatemalan people themselves, but ties student learning about the ancient Maya world to the modern one. I want my students to heighten their awareness of human rights issues in the modern countries that have grown from the older civilizations we study. I want them to think through the human rights issues for those ethnic populations in the United States, whether that has to do with child labor or the conditions under which the brand-name clothes that students wear are produced.

As I reflect on the serendipitous nature of the development of this project, sometimes I think I used too much time to explore the

Maya. However, it takes a tremendous amount of time to lay the foundation for the exploration of culture, create a language for serious inquiry, and build rigorous routines for research and collaboration. Other times, I think it was time well spent. Together we constructed a "here" from which to ask probing questions about history, culture, myth, and life.

Notes

1. Time Life's *Lost Civilizations: Maya-Blood of Kings*, prod. and dir. Joe Westbrook, 48 min., Time-Life, 1994, videocassette.
2. "The Conquest of Mexico," compiled by Irene Nicholson, Jackdaw Publications, P.O. Box AO3, Amawalk, NY 10501
3. Ibid.
4. Tedlock, D., trans. 1985. *Popul Vuh: The Definitive Edition of the Mayan Book of the Dawn of Life and the Glories of Gods and Kings.* New York: Simon and Schuster.
5. *Popul Vuh: The Creation Myth of the Maya*, produced by Patricia Amlin, distributed by the University of California Extension Media Center, 2176 Shattuck Ave., Berkeley, CA 94704.

Response from a Colleague:
Creating a Culture of Respect

Bill Fulton

Marg Costello's motif of archaeological excavation and inquiry is both a powerful model of learning and a symbol of hope for improving education, especially in urban schools. Marg reminds us that archaeology depends as much upon the ordinary as the grand. For an archaeologist seeking to understand an ancient culture, or what it means to be human, the lives of ordinary people contain as many riches as those of wealthy rulers. Unfortunately, this spirit of respect for the texture and struggles of ordinary life is something we have lost in public education. In an age of concern over the perils of our schools, we anticipate disasters or hope for immediate transformations instead of working toward gradual solutions.

Marg Costello clearly does not hold to that notion. She looks for greatness in the daily work and conversations of her students. Her description of students learning by building and testing theories against raw data unearths a vibrant classroom culture. She reveals a method of teaching and learning that inspires students to expand their understanding of themselves and the world around them, values the assets students possess, and builds on those assets to help students attain high standards of intellectual achievement.

The most striking aspect of the culture of Marg Costello's classroom is the tremendous respect she conveys for each person's ideas. "So what's the evidence?" Marg would immediately ask if I were a student in her class. It is everywhere. By beginning her exploration in the center of her students' lives, she lets her students know not only that she is interested in them, but that their lives are valuable in a grand sense. They are the point of departure for understanding what it means to be human. I imagine how it must have felt for her first day "bright-eyed, eager, enthusiastic, hormonally challenged seventh graders" to enter a new school year by presenting their own worlds to each other—pictures of family members and pit bulls, remote controls and traditional dresses. In Marg's classroom, their not-so-ordinary artifacts suddenly become evidence; their questions become hypotheses. Each student is welcomed as an expert on being human and an asset to an ongoing educational project.

Marg anticipates great things arising in her students. She devotes several days of small-group and whole-group time to discussion questions. She takes pictures of her students engaged in learning to display for their parents. In this way, students learn from the very beginning that who they are and what they do each day is valued. How different this is from the treatment so many students receive! Middle schools all over the country begin each year with uncanny uniformity, sending messages that students are empty vessels at best and, more likely, potential disrupters who need to be taught "how things work around here." The contrast between Marg's faith in students and other middle schools' fear of them is both disturbing and ironic. By fearing students' difficulties and deficits, many schools create their own burden of surveillance and control, where time is spent continually stamping out disruptions instead of creating a learning environment that makes use of students' energy. Security guards patrol the halls with crackling walkie-talkies; students are "dressed down" in front of their peers; public address systems blare out the names of "offenders." We would be wise to pay attention to what we sow.

Events like the Awareness Month that Marg describes often draw fire from a variety of critics. Some believe such events water down academics and foster a divisive "ethnic cheerleading." Although it's tempting to dismiss these charges as products of stodgy intolerance, at times they are accurate. In our efforts to include new perspectives, we sometimes crowd our curricula with broader and thinner coverage instead of promoting deeper understandings. Activity sometimes displaces learning. Marg offers a powerful response to those charges. She insists that her students accompany her on a journey below the surface of textbook coverage to appreciate the richness of cultural diversity and universality. The evidence of her success is abundant. Her student April's response to "Why study the Maya?" is a case in point. April's statement that "if I know how I feel and how I think, I can understand [the Maya] since they too are people" is the kind of budding historical empathy that makes in-depth analysis possible. April begins with an understanding of her own world and makes a connection to the broader world around her. In answering the same question, another student, Christopher Rivera, takes this connection a step farther:

> We could think what was important to the Mayas and then piece little ideas at a time until we have a picture in our minds of what they did and what was really important to them. We can also try to picture them and what they did to get an idea of how life was in Mayan civilization. We also can picture ourselves and think what we would have done and might better understand how the Maya lived.

Christopher is engaging in the same type of imaginative inquiry that any good anthropologist or archaeologist must carry out. He understands that even more than being people "just like us," the Maya had their own complex culture that can only be understood through careful analysis. Kelly Mostert points out another way to understand ourselves and others: "[Studying the Maya] can help us see how we are different from other cultures. It can also show us how we are different from our ancestors and from people of our past. If we had a list of theirs, maybe we could compare and better understand their culture, life hieroglyphics, and symbols."

The same insight and interest in the Mayan culture shows up in the list of questions that students generated as they began their explorations. When students ask questions like, "Did [the Maya] have any heroes like the Greeks?," "How did they get their position of authority?," "Why did they live in that particular area?," and "How did archaeologists figure out how to read their writing?," they are wrestling with profound questions about the nature of culture and how we study it. This is hardly a superficial treatment of cultural celebrations, nor is it divisive. Marg begins by asking her students who they are, expands the inquiry to look at who the Maya are, and ends up asking her students what it means to be human. That kind of Awareness Month can stand up to any critique.

But Marg also holds her students to the same standards as professional archaeologists. They must "make hypotheses, examine artifacts, look for evidence, listen to the evidence of the 'experts' and their peers, and then revisit and revise their hypotheses." To some, these might sound more like tasks than standards. To me, they are the most compelling examples of standards because they contain the authenticity of real life. Hypotheses face much stronger judges than teachers' pens; they must stand up to the data. Evidence is not merely a list of information, but information in relationship to a claim. When Piccola and James hypothesize about the Aztec codices, they are weaving together their background knowledge, interpretation of cultural symbols, understanding of narrative structure, and sense of what is important in life—just as other archaeologists do. So when they hear the "correct answer" from Marg, they do not simply stop thinking and accept it blindly. Instead, they want "to know how those archaeologists came to the conclusion they did." The students validate truth claims based on how well they fit the data, rather than on the authority of the person who makes them.

When students internalize high standards, they are far better equipped to take their own thinking seriously. Edwin Ramos Jr.'s response to Marg's question about Mayan timekeeping demonstrates this particularly well. After explaining how the Mayan calendar system works, he goes on to describe how his new knowledge led to questions about the similarities between the Maya number system and our own.

> The first [similarity] I thought of were the disks, when they move independently, that can be related to the way the arms on our clocks move independently and tell us the time. The second one that popped out of my head was the carvings or paintings . . . that can be related to the numbers that are

painted on the clock. Another one that I thought of was the disk. Usually disks are round and the old-fashioned way of keeping track of time was on a round disk. What similarities can you think of besides the ones I mentioned?

Edwin is not waiting for someone to interpret information for him. He is confident about his insights and connections, and invites us to add to his ideas. These examples affirm Marg's goal that her students look with a "sense of possibility and healthy skepticism" at the data and interpretations of others. These are rigorous requirements that invite students to think like archaeologists rather than merely studying what archaeologists think. This is the kind of teaching that brings standards off the wall chart and into the work that students produce.

Marg's narrative is a powerful story of what can happen when a classroom takes on a culture of its own, one infused with respect for individuals and a value for commonly developed and publicly discussed high standards. The temptation is to take her outline, enact it, and expect similar results. But as Marg's students know well, cultures are complex and do not yield their mysteries to casual study. Trying to replicate Marg's classroom activities without the supportive environment where they take place would be like trying to become a Maya by simply staying overnight in the ruins of Guatemala. Without a culture that values students, sustains learning through inquiry, and rewards bold thinking, the methods Marg describes would be powerless.

But within a culture of respect and high standards, Marg can bring to the surface qualities her students already possessed, but that might have remained unseen by other observers, just as an ordinary dish or sandal could be discarded in the search for an altar or a crown. Though she rightfully takes aim at some misuses of resiliency research, her teaching supports a central tenet of the thinking behind resiliency studies: success is a function of the assets one possesses; the greater the number of assets, the greater the chance of success. If we want all students to have a fair shot at success, then we must learn to recognize and build on the assets they already have. Marg's journey into the Maya is an exceptional example of what happens when we see students in that way. Perhaps Marg's students can help us all become better educational archaeologists, teaching us to value the ordinary treasures that are no doubt the secret to our culture's survival.

But Marg's classroom is a culture within a culture. The clue to this is in Nick Bartel's prologue. While I have written in response, Nick has written in dialogue. He midwifed the chapter—crossing all our expectations about which gender leads and which gender assists. They teach and talk together—that is clear. But this is more than pair-sharing or peer-editing. Nick can see into the heart and soul of Marg's work, much as a skilled eye reads what is in back of a painter or a poet: seeing through the shapes and colors to the motives, finding the deeply thought-out design that animates the surface. Imagine the geometric changes in city schools if we, the adults, cared and were cared for at that level.

2

We Knew Where We Wanted to Go and We Think We May Have Arrived

Phyllis McDonough Rado and Victoria Rodríguez Garvey

We teach at A. I. duPont, a small middle school (598 students) in Wilmington, Delaware, that draws a mix of urban and suburban students. Our students come to us based on where they live in order to comply with a twenty-year-old desegregation court ruling. As of the 1996–1997 school year, any student from the four districts in northern Delaware could choose to come to "A. I." The desegregation order ended this year, and a state law guaranteeing public school choice is now in effect.

When most people think about desegregation, they imagine the gerrymandering of segregation and intimidation that kept students of different ethnicities enrolled in different schools and receiving distinctly different levels of education. But for years we also tolerated what you might call "front-hall" or "split-level" segregation. If you rode the buses or watched as the students poured out of their doors into the school yard, all seemed well. But if you had entered the classrooms, you would have noticed that the bilingual students in general were segregated from the rest of the school. A. I. is the home of the middle school bilingual program for Spanish-speaking students of all four northern New Castle County school districts. These students make up about 20 percent—one in every five—of our school population. Of those hundred or so Spanish-speaking children, fewer than 5 percent—one in twenty— spent time in classes where English, a key to opportunities in school and life, was the teaching language. Any mainstreaming usually occurred in social studies, science, and math classes. Rarely, if ever, did bilingual students enter a mainstream language arts classroom—even though that might well be one of the richest environments in which to learn their second language.

Since 1991, a group of teachers from both bilingual and mainstream classes has been quietly, but forcefully, fighting to make our bilingual program an important part of our school, rather than a world apart: underserved, isolated, and unacknowledged. Our task has not been an easy one. Initially, we were up against a wall of misconceptions and barriers. Many thought of the bilingual program as little more than a baby-sitting service where no real teaching could take place. They saw the third- and fourth-grade materials—or worse yet, no materials at all—and assumed that these reflected all that was possible, not all that we had available. Bilingual students were segregated, joining the rest of the school only for living arts (gym, home economics, technical education, etc.). Few of the regular teaching staff had any training in supporting a student whose English is still developing. At that time, there was little communication between mainstream and bilingual teachers. Consequently, even for bilingual students who were capable of working in English, the expectations were very low. The school was in effect broken in two.

The changes we envisioned did not happen overnight. Instead, as teachers banded together, little by little the bilingual students began to be included: they were invited on trips, more were mainstreamed, etc. Since teachers shared students, they began to communicate and to express their views on what needed to change. In 1993, our school began a relationship with PACE with the hope of examining the opportunities being offered to all students. The PACE project contained a number of teachers who were themselves bilingual and who had a personal, as well as a professional, commitment to students who were in the process of trying to acquire English. Although we argued fiercely among ourselves over the best routes to that end, those discussions were a rare chance to speak openly and passionately about what we believed mattered and would make a difference. As a result, those of us at A. I. began to make a tougher analysis of our own situation, coming to face some of the problems within the bilingual program, not only those that came from without. We faced our need to be forceful about getting new teaching materials, no matter what the delays or difficulties were. We began to discuss whether our own expectations for our students were high enough, or just higher than elsewhere in the school.

As this discussion persisted, we decided to use our involvement in PACE to make integration and equity for the bilingual students the central focus of our reform work. In order to promote conversations among the faculty, the sixth- and seventh-grade teams began working together to develop crosscurricular units that would bring both populations of students together. At the same time, the bilingual program finally received its new funds for materials, adopted a new English as a second language (ESL) series, and decided to follow the mainstream social studies, math, and science curricula in an effort to make our curriculum equally demanding. We pushed to drive the level of mainstreaming up from under 5 percent to 20 percent. The bilingual students were welcomed in almost every class. Many teachers now work together to solve language barrier problems. For example, we have acquired translating services that allow the mainstream teachers to provide materials in the student's first language. Much has also changed in the bilingual program. Materials are now on grade level. Our assessments are designed to meet the same standards established by the state for every student. To most eyes, the bilingual program has become as challenging as the one offered to English-only students. This chapter is the story of how we used what we knew best—expectations, teaching, and learning—to breathe life into what the courts could only mandate. It is a story of gradual, but substantial change instigated, fueled, and nurtured by teachers.

Where Did We Begin?

Luckily, we had some groundwork on which we could build. In fact, our work could stand on the shoulders of two earlier projects. For several years, Amy Parker, a talented mathematics teacher, had been deeply engaged in her own personal study of the Maya. As an outgrowth of her own investigations and travels, she had developed a project that examined how and why people all over the world develop numeric and measurement systems. In that project, students looked at systems that ranged from mapping storms, to orienteering, to the numerals and place values that the Maya invented as a part of their astronomy and historical record keeping. Because of her own interest in using two languages, Parker was sensitive to the situation of the bilingual students. As a result, she made every effort to open the doors of her mathematics classes to students who could thrive there, but whose English kept them out of many other mainstream classes. In many ways, Parker's determination to straddle the two worlds was an important early symbol for what we were determined to achieve.

As the first leg of our crosscultural curriculum work with PACE, the sixth-grade English language arts teacher, Nancy Smith, and her bilingual counterpart, Mabel Saienni, collaborated on a project funded by the Delaware State Council for the Arts. In that project, bilingual and mainstream students worked side by side for six weeks creating tales in both Spanish and English that were richly illustrated with full-color collages. With the help of a talented musician and a recording engineer, students orchestrated their tales and made audio books from them. Both the large format illustrated books and the accompanying books-on-tape were contributed to bilingual kindergartens at a huge party held at the Latin American Cultural Center in Wilmington. (See Figure 2–1.) Once all the planning and celebration had died down, something very important was left standing: much of the work was strong. The texts were humorous and imaginative. The illustrations and the orchestrations were inventive. Both languages got a workout during multiple revisions. There wasn't the exhaustion that sets in after many multiplayer events. Instead, there was a sense of expectation and possibility.

As those students moved from sixth to seventh grade, the three seventh-grade teachers working with PACE were determined to keep the momentum going. We sat down with Amy Parker to lay plans. Not surprisingly, given the depth and passion of her knowledge of the Maya, we were immediately drawn to designing a crosscurricular unit that would acknowledge the highly advanced nature of that civilization compared to other cultures of its time.

FIGURE 2–1.

We immediately began tracing out the possible connections to all areas of the curriculum.

Using our language arts classes as a base of operations, we decided to integrate students from one of the mainstream classes with the students from the bilingual class. The project we developed asked students to become well versed in Mayan culture and then to write an original folktale based on their learning about the culture. The promise was large: both languages could be used for research, discussion, and developing final texts. If we were lucky, there would be direct connections to some of the bilingual students' experiences and cultures of origin, and we hoped that this personal connection would ensure that the bilingual students would become an integral part of the group. The gods—Mayan or otherwise—were with us in the first week of the project. We found ourselves eavesdropping on moments like this one, when an outside interviewer asked what students knew about the Maya as they were beginning their research (I = interviewer; BS = bilingual, Spanish-speaking student):

I: Did you know much about the Maya before this?

BS: Yeah, from my home in Mexico. Where I live there was like pyramids near to my house. We went there to have like picnics and once we went there and there were some men and they were like finding things. And they came near to my house, near to my garden and they started to bring the things out, to bring the grass out, and they found the skeletons, the skeletons that have the [?] like that. And they found jars, like big jars.

I: Were they archaeologists?

BS: Yeah, and they let everybody see them and it was kind of scary. I used to think about how they lived and it was kind of scary because they could sacrifice you. But they thought, the ones who sacrifice you, that it was an honor, that's what they thought.

Our primary goal was to integrate bilingual and mainstream students. To increase interaction between both groups, we decided to bring them together and make them depend on each other to complete their project. Our second goal was to break down some of the cultural barriers and stereotypes the mainstream students had about the bilingual students: "The bilingual students don't know anything. They can't do much. Why do we have to work with those Puerto Rican kids?" At the same time, we knew we faced equally pronounced stereotypes that the bilingual students had about the mainstream students: "The Americans don't like us. They are all racists." One reason we chose to study the Maya was that some of our bilingual students have direct connections to the Mayan culture. During this project, it was possible that these students would be seen as vital assets because of, rather than in spite of, their first languages and cultures. The rest of the group would be able to depend on them to make sure their folktales were authentic. In fact, as we hoped, one student became a resource person not only for his group but for the entire class. He checked other students' Spanish, and helped make sure details about geography, indigenous animals, and plant life were accurate. These positive interactions were our insurance that we could erode the stereotypes that students had about each other.

Our third goal was to have all students engage in the writing process to complete a structured piece of writing at a high level. To do this, students would need to apply their knowledge of the Maya to a novel setting. The students would have to draw on their knowledge of the Maya, the characteristics of folktales, and their ability to work creatively with others. We expected students to brainstorm, write, revise, conference, revise, and so on. This writing process mattered for all of our students, but it was especially important for our bilingual students, many of whom come from families where the adults and older siblings never had the opportunity to become literate in their first language.

As part of the unit, we spent three weeks studying all aspects of the Maya's culture. We designed the curriculum so students would learn about Mayan religious beliefs, their way of life, their beliefs about beauty and family, their knowledge about architecture and astronomy, and their number system. This array of knowledge gave students much to think about. One English-speaking student recalled:

> We were learning about the Maya in all our classes. So in math class, in English, in social studies. It began to make you have questions. Like we studied how strong their number system was and how it let them put down their history and make predictions with the calendar. But then they practiced human sacrifice, too. So you wondered how they could be so smart but believe in human sacrifice, too.

We also reinforced class discussion with a series of videos on the Maya. By the time we were ready to start the folktales, the students knew the importance of obsidian and jade, farming, corn, standards of physical beauty, and the Maya's beliefs about the afterlife. At first, there was the usual sort of fascination with the "popular culture" vision of the Maya. Students were glued to illustrations of human sacrifice and bloodletting. Their conversation stuck on Mayan ideas of crossed eyes and backward-slanting foreheads as marks of beauty. But it was hard to tell what was sinking in. In the weeks following the project, students were interviewed about what they had learned, and a different picture emerged. Gone was the exclusive emphasis on the gory and exotic. In its place was a detailed appreciation for the depth and complexity of Maya civilization (I = interviewer; BS = bilingual student; ES = English-speaking student):

I: So what kinds of information about the Maya did you use when you went to write your folktales?

BS: How they make pyramids every fifty-two years.

I: Why every fifty-two years?

BS: Because they had a calendar, with three little balls, and when they all lined up, it was time.

BS: It was in cycles. And they built to mark the end of one cycle and the beginning of another one.

ES: Also, the Maya have changed so rapidly, now their lives are so much different than they once were a long time ago. Because now they are very poor, they have lost control over a lot of the land that used to be theirs, and they don't have kings to protect their rights. It makes you want to know why all that change could have happened.

ES: Some people might say it is just a coincidence, but the Maya were very smart. They predicted every eclipse. Some people might just think that because they had crossed eyes as a part of their beauty that they weren't very smart. But you really have to read all about it to understand.

BS: Yes, because they could tell you where Venus was, or where a meteor might fall. And they had a lot of subterranean rooms to hide all the gold and the jade. And they made lots of stairs so that if someone tries to get it, they will get lost.

ES: All I know is that they were very advanced. They were having a heyday while Europe was totally inferior. Their civilization was so advanced that when Europe was in the Dark Ages, they could predict Venus' orbit within one day.

I: Why do you think they could be so advanced?

BS: I think it is that for a long time they didn't have wars the way Europe did.

While this instruction went on in the students' respective classrooms, we worked hard to make sure that the same teaching and learning happened in both the bilingual and non-bilingual classrooms. After learning about the lives of the Maya, we proceeded to read and study a series of Mayan folktales. Some of these were in English only, some in Spanish, and some bilingual. In this way, any group was much better off if it had both languages at its command. We compared these folktales and completed a list of characteristics that would help students develop an original and authentic Mayan folktale of their own. Students learned that most folktales explain how something came to be, that magical forces like the number three are likely to recur in various forms, that the symbols of corn and rain play an important role, and that the humble character is usually rewarded unless it was a trickster tale.

The first year of our project we worked with a heterogeneously grouped class of mainstream students (a total of thirty students) and a bilingual class (thirty students in all) whose level of English proficiency ranged from high to none at all. The students in the bilingual class came from a mix of Spanish-speaking countries in Central and South America as well as from the Caribbean. This year, however, the composition of the mainstream class changed from a heterogeneously grouped class to a homogeneously grouped class of thirty-four honors students, due largely to an administrative decision to establish an honors class. The bilingual class remained nearly the same composition except there were twenty-five students, some of whom had no knowledge of how to read or write Spanish. These students' oral language was an informal, nonstandard Spanish and a number of them had a limited knowledge of English. Both years there were students in the bilingual class who had gaps in their schooling due to economic or political problems in their home countries. Some of these students had received no formal education for as many as four years.

In the first year, there were students who went into the project with prejudiced views and came out of the project unchanged. At no time did they cooperate with their group members. We saw this happening and invited someone to the class to do a lesson on accepting cultural differences and learning from each other. One student rolled her eyes, put her head down, and actually wondered aloud, "Why do we have to have these Spanish kids in here?" Most of the groups in our first year got the work done, but few students developed relationships outside of the classroom.

We thought long and hard about what went wrong and came up with one glaring mistake. We hadn't taken the time to let the students get to know one another in a neutral setting before any work was started. Since many of the mainstream students and most of the bilingual students had been involved in similar writing projects in the sixth grade, we had cut short any "mixer" activities, assuming that most of the students already knew each other. But it was exactly the students who had not been involved in the sixth-grade project who were bogged down by their stereotypes and prejudices.

Repairing our mistake, during the second year we spent two days involving the students in mixer activities to let them get to know one another. In addition, the attitudes of the students going into the project were much more positive. They had not had a chance to do a project like this in the sixth grade, but they had heard about the project, and wanted their chance to do something similar.

When we paired the classes for the project, we put students in groups of three and four in order to give everyone an opportunity to succeed. We tried to accomplish this by grouping students heterogeneously. We took English levels and Spanish levels into consideration to ensure that all students would be equally important to the success of the group. By and large, this investment in careful group process paid off. The students also sensed the productivity of their work together:

I: How did it work out to have several of you working on the same book?
ES: Good. We all had ideas. There were three different people with different views. So there were three times as many ideas as in a one-person story.

When the students from our two classes were ready to meet their writing partners, we used the auditorium for two days and encouraged the students to spread out. Each student interviewed a partner, basing their questions on a valued object each had brought from home. It worked even for students with absolutely no English ability. They and their partners had to communicate by drawing or acting out their questions or answers. For example, Andy and Javier, who speaks no English, were interview partners. Andy was trying to get across the idea that he enjoys computers. He searched the auditorium until he found a floppy disk to demonstrate what he was talking about. Once Javier saw the floppy disk, he understood instantly. During this process, the bilingual students also had to teach the mainstream students some Spanish. Right away they tried to teach them funny idioms and phrases. Cindy, a bilingual student, taught her partners, Jilla and Jon, to say, "Mi burro es más inteligente que el tuyo." (My donkey is smarter than yours.) Jon found this phrase so humorous that he insisted it be included in their folktale.

> The next day, after the animals realized what was happening, they sent bird to get the Ah Kin for help. Bird told him of their displeasure and anger with the humans. Then, Ah Kin told bird he would come right away. Ah Kin set off to settle the dispute. When he got to the small village, he told them of the horrible things they were doing to the land. The villagers got angry and a large argument arose. "Mi burro es mos inteligente que el tuyo," the villager shouted in fury. The Ah Kin stormed out in frustration. He traveled deep into the jungle . . .

On our second day together we had a pizza party (always a hit) where the students met the rest of the group and shared what they had learned about each other. That evening they went home and wrote letters to their partners. Most of the students jumped into this assignment and didn't hold back. The mainstream students tried to use the Spanish they learned. This letter from Andrea to Sergio shows her attempts to use her newly acquired Spanish.

> September 30, 1996
> Dear Sergio,
>
> Hola! ¿Còmo Estas? I've learned a lot about you. I've learned that you and your 4 brothers and 1 sister were born in Mexico and moved here in 1994. You love to draw and play

the saxophone. Your favorite school subject is math. You are 13 years old and your favorite food is pizza. Adios. Te veo despues!

Your amigo,
Andrea

P.S. All the Spanish I wrote in the letter, I learned from you also!

The bilingual students wrote to their partners without getting intimidated by their lack of perfect English. This letter from Michelle, who had been in this country one month when we started, to Niki shows her earnest effort to communicate.

9/30/96

Dear Niki:

She have 12 years old. She have 2 brothers. I think we have same the character and she likes the music and me to. She is a good friend and she love the animals and me to. She have brown eyes like my. She like to go to camp and my to. She is a good friend.

P.S. You are cool!

Michelle

Our third day dawned—at last, a day wholly and entirely for writing. We gave all our students instructions and reminded them to use the writing process. We discussed the important decisions they had to make together. They had to determine what type of tale they would write, choose a story line, decide on characters and names, and make a very important language decision (English or bilingual). We also shared and explained the rubrics we would use to grade their folktales.

Rubric for Mayan Folktale
Group Members' Names _____
Name _____
Title and Name 10 ___
Originality (included characteristics of the folktale and the Maya) 30 ___

Revisions 20 ___
Illustrations that match the text 30 ___
Cooperation in working with partners 30 ___
Spelling 10 ___
Capitalization 10 ___
Punctuation 10 ___
Total points out of 150 ___

They were off! The next two weeks were wall-to-wall writing and revising. Some groups worked together step by step and fleshed out the story and characters as they went. Other groups had each person write an outline of a story and then they voted on the best one. The final approach adopted by some groups was to have each person write an outline and then combine them into a single story. Once the stories were written and revised, we helped the students proofread and check them for accuracy.

Students spent their third and final week making a book dummy, doing final revisions, and making the actual books, which we called codices in honor of the books the Maya made. The groups worked independently with very little need for teacher guidance. As we surveyed our rooms, the groups were totally engaged, fully organized, and intent on completing their books. This was a point for us to kick back and enjoy the students' enthusiasm and involvement with the project and each other.

After everything was finished, students filled out an evaluation of individual and group achievement. This was a way for us to monitor our observations for accuracy. We could check and make sure that what we were observing was actually what the students were experiencing and feeling.

The group dynamics were better the second year, and the communication went much more smoothly. The students were willing to experiment in their communications with one another. When one group was working on the mock-up of its codex, Katie, a mainstream student, was trying to tell Sandra, a bilingual student with almost no English, to lay out a certain page. Sandra wasn't getting the message. Katie thought a minute, pointed to the book, and said, "Nueve." Then she gestured to Sandra who quickly understood that Katie wanted her to lay out and sketch in page nine.

Most of the groups managed to keep communications open and effective as they turned to creating the text for their written stories. Almost all groups wrote the first draft together in English. Some of the students had a problem translating because they had never done it before. It took them an attempt or two—and a lot of guidance from Vicky—to realize that translations are not done word for word. Not all groups wrote in Spanish, either, because some of the bilingual students only spoke Spanish, and did not read it or write it. This is an example: Graciela's first unsuccessful attempt at translation and her second successful translation.

First attempt:
Hace mucho tiempo un sapo tenia patas bien cortas y el jaguar tenia la cola bien chiqui. [She totally skipped the second part of the paragraph.]

Second attempt:
Hace mucho tiempo habia un sapo que tenia las patas bien cortas y el jaguar tenia la cola bien cortita. Esta es la historia de como el sapo tuvo patas largas y el jaguar su larga cola.

Even when they encountered problems with their stories, most groups proved they could negotiate and continue their work using two languages. One group had an interesting folktale in which the main characters were a mongoose and a tiger. They had to do some major rethinking after they turned in a draft and we pointed out that the mongoose and the tiger were found in Asia and Africa, not Central America. Their folktale had the characteristics of a folktale (explaining how things came to be and the repeated use of the number three in characters and events), but not of the Maya worldview or ecology. We sent them to the library to research indigenous animals. They came back with a jaguar, a quetzal, and a monkey.

Another group came up with a very nineties environmental theme that had to be revised. Their original story had the animals teaching the Mayan people a lesson about how damaging the "slash and burn" method of farming was. We had to point out to them that the ancient Maya never did learn that lesson. It took this group a while, but they found a new focus for their tale. Still another group decided to explain why the robin has a red belly. After they researched the animal life of Central America, they decided to go from a robin to a quetzal bird. They wrote:

> King Jaguar ordered Bird to be sacrificed on the spot. Ah Kin said some words, then the sacrificer threw Bird toward the bloody cenote. Just as Bird was about to hit the water, the Mayan god of death, Ah Puch, gave Bird another life. Bird's stomach touched the bloody cenote, then bird flew off toward the forest. Bird noticed that his stomach was red. We call this bird a Resplendent Quetzal. All the Resplendent Quetzals that came after this have had red bellies.

Another group searched the CD-ROM and regular encyclopedias to find out if the mountains of Central America are tall enough to have snow on them. They finally got their answer by asking someone who had been there. (See Figure 2–2.)

Almost all of the groups ended up at the library at one time or other to research some fact about the Maya or Central America. Students also used their learning logs, notes, and books we had in the classroom about the Maya.

The evolution of two of the folktales are, in themselves, important parables for "how strong bilingual work might come to be." The first parable revolves around a student, Javier. In the early days of their collaboration, his group (which also included Niki, Michelle, and Andy) worked closely on their story outlines in Spanish and English to ensure that their translations were identical. After they came up with the initial story outline, they worked together to craft two matched (Spanish and English) folktales. They were careful not to revise independently as they typed in two different rooms. Each time Niki and Andy made a change in the English, one of them would go upstairs where Michelle was typing and okay it with her. Likewise, each time Michelle made a change, she came downstairs to check it with the rest of her group. We wrote so many hall passes that we finally just gave them an untimed, undated pass to use so they could travel back and forth as needed.

FIGURE 2–2.

Chac asked them to lower the mountains so the Lords did. Some of the mountains came down a little roughly and took some of the clouds down with them so that is why the mountains look different from each other and why the mountains have white on the top of them.

Chac les pregunto que tenían que hacer para que las montanas bajaran , los Dioses le respondieron que las podían disminuir un poco, entonces una pequeña parte de las nubes bajo con la montana y esto haría que se vieran diferentes a cualquier otras, y por eso las montanas tienen nieve en la punta.

But where was Javier during all of this? Javier was working solo, drawing the pictures for the book. The group tried as much as possible to pull him into writing the story, but it was difficult to get him to contribute ideas or opinions. No matter what the group tried, Javier was not willing to engage, except with his illustrations—where he wanted all kinds of artistic license. Figure 2–3, for instance, shows how he tried to contribute. While he drew the jaguar's head called for by the story, he insisted on adding the owl

FIGURE 2–3.

circling above, even though there were no owls in the story. As a student whose first language and personal history made it hard for him to engage in school, Javier had adapted by developing his skills as an artist. Although this project had much promise for connecting him to literacy in both Spanish and English, he actively shied away from being an author. It is worth wondering how his illustrations—and his artistic license—could have become a bridge, rather than a barrier, to literacy. In bilingual classrooms everywhere, there are students like Javier, who have perfected their skills as artists, caricaturists, oral speakers, performers (in all senses of that word), and leaders. These skills can become links to or ways of avoiding the hard business of becoming literate.

And then there is the parable of Erin, Sheena, Diana, and José— a group of students who had a strong beginning, but who gradually drifted apart. The mainstream students working in Phyllis's room typed on the computers they had there. The bilingual students took their drafts upstairs to the bilingual computer lab where there is a Spanish spell-checker. Erin, who is very quiet, worked on typing the story in English. Sheena, who is more outgoing and tried to coordinate everyone, was absent for several days. Diana worked upstairs typing the Spanish version, and José began the illustrations for the book. As Erin and Diana typed in their respective languages, they revised and did not think to tell the other what changes they made. The folktale, which started out the same, evolved into two quite different stories. Unfortunately, we did not catch the disparity between the two versions until the last week of the project. The group went through two days of agony and several attempts to rectify the situation before deciding—not entirely happily—to write the story in English only.

First, they tried using the school's translating program. They also tried fixing the two drafts to equalize them. Neither of these ideas worked. José, whose English is much stronger than Diana's, did not want to work on bringing the stories together. He had worked hard on the illustrations and did not want to turn his efforts to this daunting linguistic hurdle. Diana had much more invested in "fixing" the two drafts. But she was so overwhelmed by the work of bringing the two drafts together that she could not stay focused on any one solution long enough to make some progress. Erin stayed quiet and Sheena was still absent. Finally, with the stress of a fast-approaching deadline, the group decided to produce an English-only book. It was a great relief to them when we reassured them it would not "hurt" their grade. Language choice was never a part of our rubric: we wanted students to make that choice themselves. They completed their mock-up and final copy, but their experiences also left them very thoughtful about the process and the politics of working across two languages. In their interviews at the close of the project, both the mainstream (ES) and the bilingual (BS) students in this group spoke up frankly:

I: One of you was telling me that in the end your folktale was only in English.

BS: I want to use the Spanish, but Mrs. [?] say, "Oh, no, do it in English. You can do it in English. And oh and not because *they* do it in English.

ES: See, everyone in the group understands a little English, but me and Erin don't understand any Spanish.

BS: All the Spanish was right, but . . .

ES: We would tell each other what to write but it came out really different in Spanish and English.

I: If it was just a little different, did it matter that much?

ES: Yeah, because at the end we were each revising, so at the end they got really different.

I: Were the stories really that different?

BS: It means the same thing.

ES: Yeah, it meant the same thing, but the words got really different.

I: If you had had enough time, what would you guys have done?

ES and BS: Together . . . We would have probably kept it in both . . . one Spanish, one English.

ES: We had this problem that we had to read it out loud and some of them don't read English so well, so it was hard, we got through it, but it would have been better if it was in Spanish, too.

I: It is hard to make all those decisions at the end when time is running out.

BS: We could've done it, so it was very bad we ran out of time.

[Later on in the interview, another student returns to this topic:]

BS: I think that . . . I think that I want to make, you know, my own folktale, you know, because she has her own different ideas and I have my own different ideas. I want to make something and she wants to make something. And it is too difficult that everybody can like the same thing. So we can share the ideas and then make one in Spanish and one in English.

Although in retrospect the students said they would have resolved the issues differently, the whole episode, though complicated, feels like evidence of success, or at least progress. At the outset of the project, some of our Spanish-speaking students were too uncertain of their skills to risk this kind of back-and-forth discussion of differences of opinion. They might well have swallowed their concerns entirely or only shared them in the privacy of an all-Spanish conversation among peers. In this conversation they are right in there, taking turns and stating their positions in an interview conducted entirely in what is becoming a second language where they command the fluency to disagree and propose alternatives. Reading and reflecting on these interviews, one sees that the students are really struggling for exactly what we have been struggling for: the equality of the two languages.

We had earned celebration. The two classes came together to share their completed works. Each group read its story to the classes, and, of course, we had a feast! We also visited the University of Pennsylvania's Museum of Archaeology and Anthropology to see their two Mayan galleries and listen to a speaker talk about the modern-day Maya. This was a chance for our students to see actual Mayan artifacts. They were excited to see a stela and to be able to decipher some of the glyphs and numbers. Students recall the visit as an exciting confirmation that they were knowledgeable students of Mayan culture:

> I knew about the stelae, but I thought they were only as big as that door over there. I never thought they would be so tall as when we saw them in the museum.

> When I read that they had jade in their teeth, I thought it would be like a filling. But then I saw that it was all over covered. It was amazing.

> We almost flooded the speaker with questions. He could hardly get his answers out before someone else wanted to know something. I don't think he expected that from kids.

As we moved through the gallery, the students were able to identify different temples and ballcourts we had studied. They appreciated seeing the plugs used for ear decorations, the obsidian knives that they knew had been used for sacrifices, and the jade-decorated teeth. They marveled at the heavy jade ceremonial Pok-a-Tok belt. (Pok-a-Tok is the Mayan ball game.) They also enjoyed impressing the speaker with their knowledge of the Maya.

An Epilogue: How Do You Assess Such a Process?

This process of combining bilingual and mainstream students to write Mayan folktales is a strong component of our larger crosscurricular unit on the Maya. Students must combine their creativity and their knowledge of the Maya in order to write their folktales. They have to use the writing process to complete their work successfully. They must also communicate with each other on a variety of levels to get the job done and to get it done well.

The project was successful in breaking down cultural barriers. When the bilingual students were first informed that they were going to work with the mainstream students, Yahaira and Darysabel frowned and made some comments about not wanting to work with the "Americans." But in Yahaira's final reflection she wrote, "I learned that not all the white people are bad." Darysabel wrote that she was very happy with the way her group worked together and divided the work. As another student wrote in her reflection:

> I learned everything from how I put the book together to what I learned about the Maya and their society. This project was very eye-opening and caused me to experience not only learning about Mayan culture, but learning to work well with others that were bilingual.

The project is also a stepping stone toward equalizing the instruction between mainstream and bilingual students. The eloquence of the students' folktales speaks for itself. One tale in particular addresses the experience of coming to be able to read what was once unfamiliar and locked:

> Ah Caca looked doubtful but opened the book and stared into it. Soon he was transfixed by all the strange symbols but could not understand them. He began to grow sleepy. He

went deep into the jungle and fell asleep under a tree holding the book. When he woke up, he saw the Sun God rising in the east. Ah Caca cried out, "Oh Sun God! Why did you give me this book, when you didn't teach me how to understand it?" The Sun God replied, "I have work during the day! I will teach you when the moon comes out!"

Ah Caca said, "Please teach me in the next two full moons."

The Sun God said, "It's a deal! Only at night, though!"

Standing in the middle of our classrooms, hearing the murmur of work in two languages, we have a sense that this project, like those that cleared the way for it, unlocked two languages, English and Spanish, making exchange possible where once there was silence and suspicion.

How do we know that we managed to break down cultural barriers with this project? What is our evidence? Certainly we have the quality of the student writing to point to, but still, as teachers you must wonder, "Now that the folktales project is over, what will remain?" Because we were collaborating with PACE, we had the fortunate support of researchers who interviewed our students as they began and once they finished the project. In the process of transcribing the tapes, some promising evidence surfaced. Here is a sample of the conversation with one group of students at the outset of the project, just as they completed their classroom research on Mayan civilization (I = interviewer; BS = bilingual student; ES = English-speaking student):

I: Can you tell me the kinds of things that you have been learning about the Maya that you think might be useful when you come to write your Mayan folktale?

BS: About their language.

I: What is their language?

BS: Kind of like different.

I: (pause) . . . Okay.

BS: And how they make their paints.

ES: And like the kinds of games they had, like they had this ballcourt game.

I: And anything else?

ES: Well, they did some kind of weird things. Like piercing different ones of their body parts. And when they had babies they put boards on the baby's forehead so that they would grow pushed back.

I: Why did they do that?

ES: Because they thought it was attractive.

I: So have you been learning about the Maya in different classes?

ES: Yeah, like in math class for about a week we have been learning about how to write their numbers and things like that.

I: And today you are getting acquainted with each other before you go to work on your folktales?

ES and BS: Yeah.

I (to BS student): Javier, your English is really good. How long have you been speaking?

BS: For about four years.

I: All at this school?

BS: No, at another school.

I (to ES student): And Sarah, do you speak Spanish?

ES: Well, I can count and things like that, but I was very glad that I got a partner who could speak English so well, because otherwise I don't know what I would have done.

Several features of this conversation are worth noting. The turns are largely short and serial. Students do not construct meaning jointly, and their remarks do not often build on one another's but are chiefly replies to the interviewer. The Maya themselves are described as exotic and strange, more frightening or weird than compelling. Students seem apprehensive about working across languages.

Listening to the tapes of students discussing what they had learned after collaborating on the folktale and visiting the museum, several changes are immediately apparent. These are especially clear with the bilingual children. First of all, more of them speak. And they do so, convinced that they have something to add to the discussion, even if they need the help of their more fully bilingual peers to get it said. For instance, a girl is describing some of the objects that interested her on the trip they took to the museum at the University of Pennsylvania:

I: And tell me, do you think it made sense to wait to go to the museum, or do you think that you should have gone right away?

FIRST BS: No, to wait. It is more interesting that way. It is very interesting how he described it. I saw . . . como se llama..

SECOND BS: Headpiece, headress.

FIRST BS: And he showed . . . como se llama . . .

SECOND BS: Like a map?

FIRST BS: Not like a map, like with the little pyramids inside . . .

I: Oh, like a diorama?

FIRST BS: Yes, diorama with the pyramids inside of it.

In another portion of the interview, the interviewer asks students to compose an "About the Authors" panel for the jacket of a book that will feature traditional tales as well as their own. She asks what they would write that would convince book buyers that this is a book by experts:

I: How would you describe yourselves so that people would trust you as experts on the Maya?

Silence.

I: How would you convince them that it is worth the time to read your book? How do you know what you know?

BS: What do you mean? I don't understand.

I: What are you going to write on here that will convince people that this is a book by people who really understand about the Maya?

BS: You mean that what we say is important?

I: Yeah.

The student then turns to the other students and translates much of this whole interchange into Spanish for them. At that juncture, a number of them join in, using whatever English they have available to convince the interviewer that they know a good deal about the Maya.

Two things are important here. The first is the students' readiness to move between languages: whichever one can carry the meaning best, that is the one to use. The second is that students feel that it is their right or maybe even their responsibility to stop a conversation until they are certain that they thoroughly understand what is being asked. They keep questioning the interviewer until they are satisfied.

Comparison between the two rounds of interviews reveals more changes in student attitudes and understandings. In the first round, bilingual students tend to make two kinds of contributions: either highly personal information (e.g., what country they came from, for how long they have been speaking English) or factual information. In the second round, you hear them speaking up about what is on their minds. For instance, discussing the trip to the museum, a student says:

> Yes, it was so interesting in there. It makes me want to be an archaeologist when they talk about the Maya. Because it makes you think and you dream like you are really in there and everything, like inside the pyramid.

The students are also willing to evaluate the project. Nowhere is this clearer than in the discussion from the group that ended up with their folktale only in English (see page 76). Perhaps most important is the fact that when students who worked together speak to the interviewer, they collaborate. They jointly build up to a common point, elaborating on what others have said, returning to a point made earlier by someone else. In fact, this is so much the case that it is hard to pull out an extract from that conversation; it is a tightly woven fabric. We will repeat a conversation cited earlier to illustrate this point:

I: So what kinds of information about the Maya did you use when you went to write your folktales?

BS: How they make pyramids every fifty-two years.

I: Why every fifty-two years?

BS: Because they had a calendar, with three little balls and when they all lined up, it was time.

BS: It was in cycles. And they built to mark the end of one cycle and the beginning of another one.

ES: Also, the Maya have changed so rapidly, now their lives are so much different than they once were a long time ago. Because now they are very poor, they have lost control over a lot of the land that used to be theirs, and they don't have kings to protect their rights. It makes you want to know why all that change could have happened.

ES: Some people might say it is just a coincidence, but the Maya were very smart. They predicted every eclipse. Some people might just think that because they had crossed eyes as a part of their beauty that they weren't very smart. But you really have to read all about it to understand.

BS: Yes, because they could tell you where Venus was, or where a meteor might fall. And they had a lot of subterranean rooms to hide all the gold and the jade. And they made lots of stairs so that if someone tries to get it, they will get lost.

The portrait of the Maya has also changed. They are no longer seen as a strange people immured in a frozen past. They are a living people with a complex past. One student says, "But you really have to read all about it to understand." A second one comments, "It makes you want to know why all that change could have happened." And a third contributes, "Their civilization was so advanced that when Europe was in the Dark Ages, they could predict Venus' orbit within one day." These young people, some native speakers of English, others native speakers of Spanish, are linked by working on a common project designed to give them equal opportunities to learn.

Response from a Colleague

Virginia Vogel Zanger

"I learned that not all the white people are bad," concludes Yahaira, a bilingual program student, at the conclusion of the Mayan curriculum unit described by her teachers, Phyllis McDonough Rado and Victoria Rodríguez Garvey. This comment illuminated for me the importance of the work described in their chapter, "We Knew Where We Wanted to Go and We Think We May Have Arrived." Yahaira's comment reflects the isolation and stigmatization that is the norm for too many bilingual students in schools across the country, well-documented in a national study of immigrant students.[1] In my own teaching and research with bilingual high school students, I found that the low status of the bilingual program and the racial hostility experienced by bilingual students can delay mastery of English and undermine academic achievement.[2] Far too rarely do students learning English have either the opportunity or the motivation to struggle to communicate with native English-speaking peers as did Michelle, the recent immigrant whose letter is included in the essay.

Yahaira's comment is also significant because it underscores how effective the collaborative curriculum unit was in transforming her attitudes. Apparently, it had a similar impact on the monolingual program students as well, as one student reflected on what she had gained from the unit: ". . . not only learning about Mayan culture, but learning to work well with others that were bilingual." The opportunity for students to develop what might be termed intercultural proficiency is one of the most compelling features of this unit. Although their school was racially desegregated with presumably great cost and effort, it was by no means integrated. Therefore, the careful structuring of the unit to allow students to get to know each other, find out what they had in common, and learn with and from each other is extraordinarily important.

The teachers developed the Mayan unit after a careful analysis of the lack of integration and equity in their school. The design of the unit brilliantly addresses both issues. Far too often, efforts to integrate bilingual and monolingual program students throw students together in situations that place bilingual students at a clear disadvantage. The teachers' decision to introduce collaboration only after each group had had the opportunity to learn about the subject matter first in their native language leveled the playing field. So did the nature of the subject matter itself, for it provided the bilingual students a genuine opportunity to serve as experts. Moreover, the activities were carefully structured to address the equity issue. Bilingual students must be given opportunities to show what they know beyond the usual English literacy context. Therefore, Rado and Garvey made sure students could express their ideas through writing in Spanish and drawing. Although the authors are disappointed that the unit did not engage one bilingual student, Javier, to participate as much as they would have liked in the work of his group, the unit did allow him to make other significant contributions: beautiful drawings for his group's fable, which were no doubt highly appreciated by his peers, and his firsthand knowledge of Mexican sites relating to the class' Mayan studies. Thus, Javier's participation was not limited because of his lack of English literacy.

It is worth noting that though the unit was developed by teachers in response to the particular needs at their school, it also corresponds to the three characteristics of schools that produce the most academically successful language minority students. According to a study of 42,000 language minority students in schools across the United States, the largest ever undertaken in this country, Thomas and Collier[3] found that by high school, the language minority students who were achieving the highest (in English) had had these three features in their earlier schooling:

1. Cognitively complex academic instruction through students' first language for as long as possible and through second language for part of the school day. The intellectual sophistication of the Maya unit, including literary, geographical, historical, and scientific material, is certainly complex, and it allowed students to learn through both their languages.
2. Use of current approaches to teaching the academic curriculum through both languages, through active discovery and cognitively complex learning. Rado and Garvey's project-based unit, which relies on cooperative learning, students' synthesis of information to create a myth of their own, and the activation of prior knowledge, reflects current state-of-the-art approaches to teaching.
3. Changes in the sociocultural context of schooling, e.g., integration with English speakers, in a supporting, affirming context for all; an additive bilingual context, in which bilingual education is perceived as the gifted and talented program for all students; and the transformation of majority and minority relations in school to a positive school climate for all students, in a safe school environment. It is this feature of the unit, perhaps the most difficult for schools to achieve, to which the comment by Yahaira attests.

A bilingual high school student once said to me, "How can they expect students to get along when the bilingual and monolingual program teachers don't even talk to each other?" In that context, I suspect that the impact of Rado and Garvey's collaboration on their students cannot be underestimated. Certainly it was beneficial to see teachers modeling the kind of intercultural cooperation that they expected of their students.

The students also benefited from the cyclical planning process that characterized their teachers' collaboration: planning, implementation, reflection, refinement, replanning, etc. The second year that the Mayan unit was taught, it clearly went much better, in large part because the teachers had committed the time to reflect on their practice, refine it, and improve it. Rado and Garvey's account of the development of their unit is a compelling argument for structuring common planning time for bilingual and monolingual program teachers into the school day. I wondered when they found the time to do all their planning and reflection. The refinement of the unit speaks to the importance of teachers' allowing time for both. Rado and Garvey's discussion of what worked and what didn't following the first year of teaching their collaborative unit clearly led to improvements in their second year.

The main improvement that the teachers came up with was to spend two days helping students get to know one another at the outset of their collaboration. It certainly seems to have made a big difference in the quality of work that students ultimately did, as evidenced by the folktales, as well as in the quality of students' interaction. The time invested setting up good working relationships paid off for the same reason that cooperative learning works best when time is allotted for explicit development of social skills. Students are not computers to be programmed with curriculum and standards, no matter how well designed; they learn in a social context. If we expect them to learn from and with each other, we must spend some time establishing and nurturing those relationships.

Rado and Garvey felt that much of the success of their second year teaching the unit was due to the "icebreaker" activities that they developed for students. Though these activities did help students to connect personally and feel comfortable, they were by no means trivial, feel-good time wasters. The heart of these activities was the one-on-one interview of a peer from a different cultural and linguistic group. When I taught high school to bilingual students, I found this to be such a powerful pedagogical technique that I eventually wrote a book for students that addresses learning about other cultures by interviewing peers.[4] When Rado and Garvey teach the unit again, they could push the interview technique even further, using it as a way to include parents. Students from Mexico and Central America could interview their parents or members of their communities about various aspects of Mayan legends, history, and culture.

Another extension that Rado and Garvey might incorporate when the class is taught again would take advantage of the personal relationships developed during the unit by using them as a way of improving students' literacy. In the second year of the unit, Andrea and Michelle's letter exchange was an impressive example of how students will push themselves to write in their second language if they are sufficiently motivated. Why not encourage further correspondence—by letter or email—after the unit ends?

I was so impressed by the Maya unit that I shared the chapter with a friend who teaches ESL and seventh-grade English. She recalled a collaboration along similar lines undertaken by two colleagues in Brookline, Massachusetts, who paired a Russian bilingual class and a middle school English class for the study of a literature unit on Gogol, Pushkin, and Chekhov. My friend, however, was overwhelmed by the planning demands of these impressive efforts. We talked about ways that bilingual and monolingual program teachers could begin collaborating in smaller ways. One place to start is with structured peer interviews, as described by Rado and Garvey. Social studies classes studying immigration, the history of bilingual students' countries of origin, or comparative governments could interview bilingual students. Another natural pairing is between foreign language classes and ESL students who are native speakers of the target language. I suspect that as teachers discover—as I did—students' excitement about crosscultural explorations with peers, they will look for ways to expand and extend these activities. Rado and Garvey's work stands as an excellent model for doing so.

I commend the authors on their work and urge other teachers to try similar collaborations between bilingual and monolingual program classes. Despite a certain lip-service to the benefits of global education, students from other parts of the globe are rarely used as a resource and often find themselves isolated in school. Rado and Garvey's solution is particularly significant in light of the political winds currently sweeping through education. The organized and well-funded campaigns of the English-only movement, the battles over whose history to include in social studies curriculum standards and whose literature to include on required reading lists, and the increasing trend toward the privatization of education all threaten to deepen the inequities experienced by bilingual students—and deprive monolingual program students of opportunities to learn about the world. Sadly, it is often left to teachers to try to undo the damage wrought by politics outside their control. Rado and Garvey have risen to the occasion.

Notes

1. National Coalition of Advocates for Students (NCAS). 1988. *New Voices: Immigrant Students in U.S. Public Schools.* Boston: NCAS.
2. Zanger, V. V. 1987. "The Social Context of Second Language Learning: An Examination of Barriers to Integration in Five Case Studies. Unpublished doctoral dissertation, Boston University. Zanger, V. V. 1994. "Not Joined In: The Social Context of English Literacy Development for Hispanic Youth." In B. M. Ferdman, R.M. Weber, and A. Ramirez, eds. *Literacy Across Langauges and Cultures*, Albany: State University of New York Press.
3. Thomas, W. P., and Collier, V. P. 1977. *School Effectiveness for Language Minority Students*. Washington, D.C.: National Clearinghouse for Bilingual Education.
4. Zanger, V. V., 1993. *Face to Face: Communication, Culture, and Collaboration*. Boston: Newbury House/Heinle & Heinle.

3

Like a Puzzle

Tammy Swales Metzler

"Oh, you mean this is like a puzzle—you want us to put the pieces together . . ."

About Puzzles and Puzzling

You ponder a display of puzzles. All of the boxes are colorful and intriguing; all lure you to buy, to see if you can meet their challenge. You contemplate, waiting for one to jump off the shelf. The picture becomes all important—who wants to spend hours and all that "puzzling" on a project that doesn't challenge you intellectually, emotionally, and visually?

So you take your pick and bring home your puzzle. You dump it out onto the table and pause in dismay. There are a million oddly shaped pieces! How will you ever complete that enormous picture? Suddenly you realize it's the *puzzling* that's the real attraction: the strategies you will employ to complete the task. Perhaps you'll begin with color, piecing together islands of blue or speckled-green. Maybe you will work with shape, locking each unique contour into its precise partner pieces, like keys fitting into locks. Or maybe you will use edges, looking for all the pieces that have at least one flat side.

But what if these hands-on, immediate clues are nowhere near enough? Imagine that the picture you chose is a view of the temples and squares of Tikal, one of the great Mayan archaeological sites. Most of the thousands of pieces are gold, green, and brown; many are similar in shape; and only a few have a flat edge. So, unless you are going to work slavishly from the picture on the box, or doggedly try every piece as the mate for every other, your success is going to depend on being able to observe, make connections, imagine possibilities, even form hypotheses. You might think:

> Green and black jungle terrain . . . palm ferns maybe . . . so this could be the edge of the surrounding forest . . . and this one here looks like a paw carved into the stone . . . could belong to one of those jaguars you see along the temple walls . . . wait, where was that one piece I just saw, the one with the stripe running through it, the one I thought was a stair, maybe it's the tail?

Being Able to Puzzle

Why all of this about puzzles? Because for me, puzzles are a powerful image for both educational business-as-usual and education as it might be. I work in a city and a school where many students' learning is challenged: our school has the highest level of poverty in our district. Kids walk to school with no breakfast, no coats, no boots to protect them against the harsh winter. When it's bitterly cold, our school closes, not because the roads are so terribly bad, but because our kids could freeze in their thin coats. Students are sometimes followed and harassed on their way to school, not only by other students, but by adults, whose frustration with their own poverty and joblessness spills over onto our students.

Much too often, adults misread the difficulties and challenges students face, attributing problems in school to "students with learning problems," or "students who are slow," "dumb," or "angry." "They can't" is a phrase I hear all the time, either out loud or as a quiet undercurrent. On several occasions, after describing what students are doing in my class, I have been dismayed to hear teachers sniff disdainfully and actually say, "Well, that's okay for *you*, but those little animals I have upstairs would never be able to do that. I wouldn't even give them the opportunity." In short, many of the students I teach are not seen as candidates for stepping up and choosing a big or tough puzzle. Instead, they are often handed a simple "six-piecer" to be cut from a worksheet and assembled using step-by-step directions: *Step one: Cut all pieces apart. Do not cut dotted lines. Step two: Color the pieces labeled with a "1" pink. Step three: Glue the pieces onto a heavy sheet of paper.* I constantly wonder how they can ever grow an appetite for hard puzzles, based on such a steady diet of fake challenges, stubby clues and lock-step strategies.

I want students, even those I only pass in the hall, to puzzle. I want them to be engaged and confident enough that they reach out for the biggest, subtlest picture, I want them to go to it armed with a whole toolkit, and use every bit of knowledge and savvy they have. I want them to piece big answers together, acting as detectives, laboratory scientists, and archaeologists. Unfortunately, getting there is not that simple.

My students are smart—no question. Give them a question or a problem and they intuitively "get it." When I began teaching them about the Maya, I showed them a big, dark circle on a piece of paper and explained that this symbol was very important to the Maya. Then I let them brainstorm on what they thought this "dot" could be.

What could this be, and why is it significant to the Maya?

The Sun	A Circle of Life	An Egg
The Moon	Death	Space
The World	Hieroglyphics	God
Time	Eternity	Mark of Honor
Signature	A Culture Sign	Togetherness
Unity	King's Mark	Marriage

Clearly their responses showed that they intuitively knew some things about culture, people, and the value that is placed upon certain symbols. But going from a hunch to an answer takes methods, strategies, persistence, patience, and high standards. In the mysterious territory where intuition turns to rigorous thinking, all of us—my students and myself—had to roll up our sleeves.

I spent a number of years assuming that kids were thinking in my classroom. Students were doing what I asked them to do, repeating what I had taught to them on their tests, and participating in class discussions to the extent I demanded. I felt I was being a successful teacher. My kids were doing what I asked them to, right? When I first began teaching world history, I started with dinosaurs, rushed past early man painting mysterious symbols in caves, leaped into ancient Egyptian dates and pharaohs, tackled the fall of Rome, showed a few semirelated videos (Cleopatra comes to mind), rushed through the Middle Ages, and landed neatly in the Industrial Revolution and the World Wars. My students dutifully practiced that well-known procedure of "answering the questions at the end of the chapter." No *thinking* was allowed. The problem was, I was bored. My students? *Of course* they were bored—they were always bored—but they were *productive*. So how wrong could I be?

I noticed that at certain times during this mad historical (hysterical?) rush through history my students *were* interested. They liked looking at cuneiform and hieroglyphics, imagining what castles were like, thinking about the battles that were an inevitable part of life then. I began to wonder if perhaps there might be a way to *engage my students in world history as an opportunity to get them to think*, make connections, and hypothesize why and how. I wanted to use writing and numerical systems across cultures as a possibility to engage students, but I was afraid that students would not be "into it." I began taking tentative baby steps to move away from rote learning of facts and dates, and into the murk of engaging my students' minds in inquiry. I started asking for their opinions on things—and boy, did I ever get them! I discovered that first I had to tackle my own confusion regarding inquiry before I could explain it to and expect it from my students.

Being invited to participate in the curriculum seminars in collaboration with Harvard PACE gave me the opportunity to begin developing some of my ideas about putting complex tasks into actual practice. During this series of seminars we, as teachers, had the opportunity to immerse ourselves in a civilization: That of the Maya from Central America. Our objective was to apply our newly acquired knowledge and insight to create experiences for our students that would allow them to become thinkers and problem solvers.

During a visit to the Peabody Museum in Cambridge, a practicing archaeologist challenged us to examine a dot. He was offering us one piece of a puzzle, only it was perfectly round—no flat edges, no other pieces to compare it to. And there was no picture on the cover of the box. We were asked to hypothesize what the dot represented, and build theories about what it was and why it had been so significant to the Maya. Feeling intimidated and unsure of what I was supposed to do, I became the quiet student in the back. A year later, I would challenge my students to answer this same question, but at that particular moment my own sense of frustration flared. I felt stuck. My past experiences didn't seem to connect—if you will excuse the expression—to the dot. As the facilitator introduced more pieces—other dots and bars—I couldn't for the life of me see the pattern everyone else was perceiving so easily! Eventually, once I was given enough clues, I did come to some sort of conclusion about the dot and what it represented to the Maya. But that same sense of frustration was to come back to me throughout my own search to find a way to immerse my students in the culture of Mayan civilization. Reading about it in two paragraphs in a text book had been so easy. . . . .

When I went back to my classroom, I was eager to try the activity with students. As their comments show, my students certainly generated some interesting responses about what the dot could represent. But then we stalled. They couldn't readily connect the pieces and explore the larger place of the dot in Mayan culture. They had no way to assemble the picture on the cover of the box. I ended up having to tell them about it, and a lot was lost in translation. Again, I was doing the thinking, and they were doing the listening. I promised myself that the following year I would try again, but this time I was determined to let students think it through for themselves.

Next year came—the way it always does: "Okay, great responses to the dot! Let me share with you other ways the dot appears in Maya artifacts and tell me what you think."

I was amazed by my students' responses: "Could it be a number? Look at the way it appears over and over. Is it words? It could be a story, because the dots and bars are not always the same—some go up and some down. I think it's a code. Could it be math?"

And then the breakthrough, coming from a quiet student who was usually hesitant to share her ideas: "Look at the patterns: the symbols wouldn't keep repeating in different ways if it wasn't letters or numbers!"

In retrospect, I wish that I had pushed her a little harder about her thinking and connecting on this.

Students tested their theory; they puzzled: "If it were letters, there would have to be more, right? Is that all there are, Ms. Swales? A dot, a shell, and a bar? I think they're numbers. What if that dot was one, two dots equal two? What about two dots and a bar then? Ms. Swales? What do you think? What's the bar mean?"

Teaching kids to think is something we all assume we are doing in the classroom. But teaching kids thinking skills, by which I mean *observing, making connections, looking for patterns, and extrapolating information from observable data*, is something we do less of. During our three-year conversations at PACE and the curriculum seminars, the issue of how much information to give kids up front before they could begin theorizing about a culture was something we all struggled with. Do we "teach" kids about the Maya, giving them lots of reading and background information before they begin making connections and looking for patterns? I kept thinking about my own experience with the dot. I really wanted my students to gain a view of cultures not as collections of artifacts and monuments, but as thought patterns, commitments, and imaginations. The struggle to understand another culture should be richer than just showing students another "us" in a different time and place. Yes, I wanted my students to think like scientists, but not at the risk of missing the poetry, beauty, and intelligence of another people.

I was determined to use the concept of thinking as the thread that wove together all of the separate pieces of the Maya that we would study. I wanted my students to reflect on the Maya and the thinking of these people. I struggled with how to use artifacts—the jewelry, the jaguar, and the great radial calendars—as inroads to a deeper understanding of the Maya, not just a collection of exotic "stuff." My challenge became facilitating my students' move from *tangible* (artifacts) to *intangible* interpretation (thinking). I wanted my students to take all the tangible pieces of the puzzle and *re-create it*, yielding understandings that were new and insightful.

The reality of the classroom, however, makes such things easy to say and much harder to do. If I were reading about a teacher who "challenged" students to become thinkers, I would be skeptical, to say the least. I know from experience that my students challenged me to become a thinker *first*.

One of the things I find most wonderful and irritating about urban middle school kids is their absolute need to get to the heart of what they are expected to do. Many of them have so much going on in their lives that they have little time or patience left for lengthy explanations and esoteric language. "Just tell us what we're supposed to do, Ms. Swales," or "Why do we have to do this?," "Why is this so boring?," "Can't we do worksheets instead of all this thinking stuff? It's too hard!" My students are often openly impatient with schoolwork that doesn't fit into their lives, and they have a collective internal meter for detecting what fits and what doesn't. I struggled against those meter readings for a long time. Often my "best" assignments—even my projects—came up short. It was hard to hear students ask questions about the what and why. It took me a while to see that *those questions were proof that my students were thinking!* In fact, those questions became my own internal meter as I planned the Maya curriculum. It would be meaningful, meaty, concrete, and engaging. When students asked their questions about the who, what, and why, I wanted to help them find the answers for themselves, and I wanted those answers to ring truer than the "because you have to" response they've grown accustomed to.

I began my quest to develop curriculum with these guidelines in mind: I would teach students that complex tasks are only a series of smaller tasks (the puzzle pieces!) that accumulate into a larger whole. I would give them the opportunity to explore new ideas, look for meaningful patterns, and apply them in ways that are real and relevant. I didn't care if students became color-sorters, shape-examiners, or edge-people; I just wanted to create ways that enabled them to connect the pieces into a meaningful picture.

I needed a framework, a handle, or an image that could engage my students in thinking. I chose Howard Gardner's theory of multiple intelligences,[1] hoping to use his concepts as a way to help my students look at both themselves and the Maya as intelligent in many ways—a student is not only good at math, and the Maya were not only logical. I saw Gardner's theory as a tool for complexifying, rather than simplifying or caricaturing. I hoped that my students would come to understand that the Maya were intelligent in multiple ways. Given the many forms of evidence we would examine—numerical systems, temples, athletics—we would reach a more layered, diverse understanding of the culture. Examining the Maya as complex thinkers would allow students to investigate the evidence of thought in another culture and gather it into one (very large!) place. By using the framework of multiple intelligences, my students would have the opportunity to see that all thought is not identical: it comes in multitudinous forms. It would create a theater in which students could cast themselves as unique thinkers who have their own strengths.

This was the "picture on the puzzle box" that I wanted to entice students to try. I wanted them to examine and interpret a culture, forming their own conclusions from varied evidence. I wanted them to become scientists: to look for information, draw inferences, and present and justify their hypotheses both in writing and before an audience. I wanted them to become immersed in the Maya—but not superficially. When I teach my students multiple intelligence theory, it is not to validate the simplification of my students' learning: "Oh, she's visual-spatial, let her draw her ideas," or "It's Wednesday, time to be bodily-kinesthetic"—both wretched conceptions. Rather, I want them to expand their thinking and use a variety of techniques to show evidence of learning. And, in the end, I wanted them to show off their new understandings in a challenging performance assessment that would reflect all that they had learned to do.

Introducing students to the investigative and questioning techniques of archaeology and encouraging them to use those techniques themselves were important on-ramps to immediate engagement in the scientific process of examining evidence, as well as creating and following up on hypotheses. Throughout the school year I gave my students three tasks from which they learned to extrapolate information about cultures:

1. examining modern artifacts to imagine what others might think of our culture a thousand years hence
2. reading an Egyptian hymn and transferring their knowledge about both Egyptians and "hymn words" to create their own "hymn to the Nile"
3. looking at castle floor plans and predicting what life must have been like in the Middle Ages

By spring, they had the building blocks to work on the Maya project. Together, we were headed into new uncharted territory to think about thinking.

So we began, not with the Maya, but with the students themselves. My entry point was simple, immediately relevant, and accessible to everyone. I asked students to describe what learning "looked like." Their answers were not unexpected: "You're listening . . . taking notes . . . reading . . . quiet." I could smell the constraints of schoolbound thinking. "Aha!" I said. "What about describing for me a time when you were not in school and you learned how to do something? What did learning look like then?"

Students rumbled and put their heads together. When at last they responded, their answers ranged from rollerblading to plumbing to cooking. They recognized that such learning didn't necessarily look like learning did in school. There was usually someone involved who supported them through the process. I had learned to teach about thinking: to pose genuinely open questions and to support the development of serious answers over time—no rushing in to do the puzzle for them. My students put the skill to immediate use and kept it at a high polish. They wanted to learn because it was important, fun, even exhilarating:

How I Learned to . . .
My sister, neighbors, and mom was there.
I felt excited, nervous, and scared.
My sister already had her Rollerblades since Christmas.
First, I learned to stand straight on my feet.
Then, I learned to glide, turn, and steer, and stop.
After I learned, I felt the urge to scream and glide all over
Rochester, N.Y.

I thought I was going to fall and kill myself like riding a bike.
I fell on my back—I got up and felt like quitting—
but I didn't.
ROLLERBLADE

—Eugene

We explored the conditions under which significant learning takes place, with students taking charge of the language:

Expectation: You expected to learn, so you did!
Immersion: Jump into the experience—JUST DO IT!!
Use: You use the skill right away.
Engagement: You are interested and involved in the learning.

Together, what we realized was sameness in difference. As different as Eugene was in gender, history, family, and skills from some of his classmates, there was much about his process of learning that was universal. Now we were ready to take the question of learning across cultures.

So my curriculum began, not with a lesson about the Maya, but with a lesson about seventh graders. Why is that important? I wanted to show them that the capacity for learning is universal. By working together to define learning, everyone was engaged—and everyone had already had a learning experience!

To expand on the students' interest in their own process of thinking and learning, I introduced them to the idea that learning can happen in more than one way—that there are multiple paths to learning, some of which unfold outside of school. I introduced students to the idea of multiple intelligences. We explored the very different ways that they make sense of their experience:

- Sometimes when I'm mad I like being alone and just thinking and daydreaming to myself.
- Whenever I read a book I can always visualize a picture inside my head. Having visual-spatial as one of my strong intelligences helps me to be more descriptive and creative when I speak and write.

Then came the big leap: based on their previous study of ancient civilizations, I asked my students whether they could use what they knew about the multiple intelligences to help them understand a culture or civilization different from their own.

Students were immediately responsive: "YES! We can!" I asked for examples, even though I wasn't sure what kind of responses I would get. After a long pause one student raised his hand. "If you found bones buried somewhere and the groups of people were found close together, you could say they were interpersonal, but if they were separated they might be intrapersonal." Wow. That answer went above and beyond my wildest dreams of greatness! The students were off and running as we generated a beginning list.

Found items	Intelligences those items demonstrate
Tools	Logical
	Visual-spatial (visualizing what they look like before they are made)
	Bodily-kinesthetic (making them and using them)
Drums	Musical-rhythmic
	Bodily-kinesthetic
Pictures	All seven!
	Verbal-linguistic (to communicate)
	Mathematical-logical (patterns)
	Interpersonal (more than one artist?)

I had students hooked, and I wanted to keep them there. I had been frustrated at times when I myself was a student of the Maya at the curriculum seminars. During our ongoing conversations as teachers reflecting on how it felt to be learners, the question of how much information to give students before they began formulating hypotheses about the Maya kept coming up. How does a teacher decide what is enough? At what point should students have the freedom to try things out, find answers, and formulate more questions? How much information should be prerequisite knowledge? I definitely didn't want to be the sole keeper of information—students needed to understand the major artifacts and theories of Mayan civilization—but I felt that I needed to find a way to frame the information about the Maya so that students also took ownership of the *process* of discovery and information.

A culminating event, the Archaeological Center of Maya Research Symposium, was what I came up with as the concrete way for my students to assume their roles as archaeologists and thinkers. (See Figure 3–1.) From the start I forecasted a formal occasion during which students would be asked to use the language of archaeologists, thinkers, and scientists to present their theories and research about a rich and complex culture. I wanted to create an environment in which the experts would share what they knew during a major event. I wanted to ensure that each student would function as both presenter and expert panelist, creating a rich tapestry of evidence gathered from more than one perspective. I wanted students to hear and reflect on each other's opinions, based on their own research and findings. In addition, I wanted them to create hypotheses about things that have no right or wrong answers, to examine artifacts as evidence in support of their hypotheses, and to think independently about a complex and interesting culture. Each student was expected to:

- conduct on-site research from data and artifacts gathered from multiple sources
- create "teaching" exhibits that would help others to understand how a culture can be explored and examined through the various intelligences
- present and defend findings in front of a leading "panel" of Maya experts

Once the "end was in sight" for both myself and my students, it became clear (at least for me!) what needed to happen at the beginning. Clearly my students needed some basic knowledge of Maya culture as we now understand it. As we began the learning process, I often needed to reassure my students. "Ms. Swales, do you know the answer to this problem?" "Guess what? There is no right answer!" When I said this, you could see the pressure drop right off of the students' shoulders. They understood that they had to take a stance based on what they believed.

For four weeks, students examined Mayan number, numerical

FIGURE 3–1.

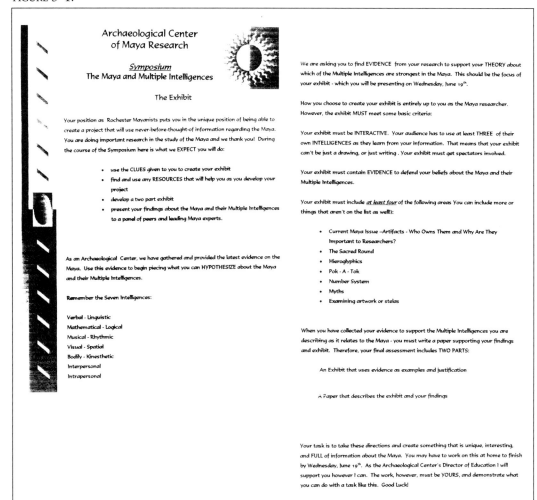

writing, and calendrical systems. I learned that one problem with teaching about culture is that it's difficult to make distant times and places real to kids; the *Voyage of the Mimi II* video series[2] and a software program called MayaQuest14 helped students' understanding tremendously. The thirty-minute videos, taped on-site at various Maya ruins, explain major theories about the Maya in extremely accessible ways, and helped make the "discovery" part of the process more real. The MayaQuest software was a game that students used to do a "virtual walk" through the Mayan ruins around Central America, looking for clues and patterns to support their burgeoning theories about how the Maya thought and imagined. The vivid images helped them gain perspective; they could "physically" climb to the top of the temple and look around.

Using the multiple intelligences proposed by Howard Gardner as a framework, they examined artifacts as evidence for how the Maya applied their thought and formed hypotheses about their civilization. Constant revision and arguing were evident as more information was explored and internalized by students. Their beginning inferences were simple:

> There were lots of jobs. The Maya had to work with someone else on all jobs that were interpersonal, and they had to use their bodily-kinesthetic intelligence to move and lift things . . ."
>
> *—Gerrell*

Going beyond this was a steep climb. We needed to work together to read the more complex artifacts. For example, when students examined the glyphs, they were indignant that the pictures were so "weird" and difficult to understand. They didn't seem to look like anything at all, just a bunch of "squares and squiggles," as one student described it. We needed to stand in the shoes of generations of glyph makers and users. In order to aid the process, I had them draw an image of something important to them, then take that image and draw it over and over as quickly as possible. What happened—luckily! I wasn't sure it would—was that student drawings became more and more stylized.

It was then easier for them to understand that the hieroglyphics were stylized pictures of symbols, unique to another culture, as well as to a particular "artist." Once they realized this, they were able to see the faces, hands, and pictures more readily.

Finally, after spending many days with the artifacts and learning to interpret and understand them as much as possible, my students voyaged out as Mayanists to create their own theories about the Mayan mind that made such a complex civilization "tick." I created a Maya Symposium Orientation Day in which students were given artifacts (as many pictures, videos, software, readings, and resources as I could gather), an overview of the project's expectations, and a time line. Students worked individually for several days developing, supporting, and creating a presentation of their theories. It was very intense for all of us. Students struggled to make sense of my directions—I had a clear picture of what I wanted them to end up with—but the process proved difficult to facilitate. Students kept asking if they should choose one intelligence to focus on, and I kept explaining, writing, and drawing ways that I wanted them to think about the many kinds of intelligence for which they had found evidence. Here is one student's draft as we edged toward understanding:

> I feel that the Maya were strong in four of the seven intelligences: bodily-kinesthetic because they were strong, built pyramid-temples over 200 feet high, and also strong in a physical aspect, too, which was demonstrated in a ball game played with a solid rubber ball in a specially made court. They were visual-spatial because they built many structures that were symmetrical. Other cultures built bigger temples, but they did not show the time and effort put into it as the Maya did with hand-crafted statues and stone-work. They were intrapersonal because most things were based on the strong spirit and mental abilities of a person and their connections with the gods, for example. And finally, the proof we have that the Maya were thinkers are the stories and myths which were well thought out and that they kept track of movements of the sun and stars.
>
> —*Thomas*

Toward the end of the process there were quite a few "ahas!" with each student developing his or her own "take" on the Maya. For instance, Gerrell found his favorite clue to Mayan culture in the recurring symmetry of Mayan sculpture and design:

I think the Maya were thinkers. . . . The proof that they were thinkers—they were strong in logical-mathematical and visual-spatial. These two intelligences connect to one thing: symmetry.

Symmetry means that things are the same on either side. I think that the symmetry the Maya used honored their gods and created a sense of order and pattern. For example: temples, glyphs, calendar, and myths.

First, the temples and calendar. When a temple was built everything had to be symmetrical, such as if they put a carved mask on one side they had to put the same carved mask on the other side. Now, the calendar. The calendar was symmetrical also because the numbers on the calendar only went up to 13 and back over to 1 again.

Second, the glyphs and the myths. The glyphs were even symmetrical a little. When they put dots on the left side they put one on the right side. [Gerrell means the small, decorative dots, not the dots that represent numbers] Finally the myths—the Maya story had to have a pattern for the story to make sense.

The idea of symmetry related to the two intelligences: logical-mathematical and visual-spatial. All this supports my opinion of why the Maya were thinkers, because it takes a lot of thinking to get nearly everything symmetrical.

—Gerrell

Another student, Candace, created a chart for her symposium project. On the chart she compared how the Maya exhibited the multiple intelligences to how American culture exhibits them today.

My name is Candace Morse and I am a Mayanist from New York. I am going to give you all the proof that I have that the Maya were thinkers. And then I am going to compare our culture to the Maya's culture to show how we too are thinkers in some of the same ways as the Maya. I have a different example for each one of the multiple intelligences. The green writing tells about the Maya and the red, white and blue writing tells about us.

Here's what this approach allowed Candace to appreciate about the Maya:

Intelligence	The Maya	Us
Visual-spatial	The stelae were sort of like statues that the Maya made to tell stories or myths or just as pictures of the lords and Gods. On the stelae were hieroglyphic writing. The Maya would fit little pictures into round square shapes, and then they're all put together to say something. To do that takes a good eye. That is an example of how the Maya were visual-spatial.	Today, many people like to do graffiti art. That is proof that we are visual-spatial.
Verbal-linguistic	The Maya number system was based , on 20 just as ours is based on 10. The numbers consisted of bars, dots and shells. The bars = 5, the dots = 1, and the shell took up space, the same way 0 does. The Maya system also had our words that are complicated. 1 is "hun," 2 is "ka," 3 is "ox," etc. The Maya number system is an example of written and spoken language, which is evidence that the Maya used their verbal-linguistic intelligence.	We also have a number system that proves that we are verbal-linguistic thinkers.
Logical-mathematical	The "Sacred Round" was one of the Maya calendars (there were 3 of them). It had 20 different named days in one month and 13 numbers, so the numbers 1–7 were used twice in one month. The Sacred Round is an example of using patterns and numbers which is evidence that the Maya were logical-mathematical.	We have a calendar that also shows that we are logical-mathematical thinkers.

As my students struggled to create unique, individual puzzles, I struggled as well. The pieces I was creating didn't fit as neatly as I'd hoped; the picture on the box was somehow distorted when I put it together. I wish that I had given myself more time to help students through the independent part: they were rushed, and their final projects reflect that. I was excited by the beginnings of understanding and nuance that students were bringing to the project. The next time around, I want to push them a little harder to "say it out loud" so I can capture the process of their thinking. Some of those opportunities were definitely lost. There are lots of gaps in the Maya puzzle—for me as well as for the students.

But despite the half-formed puzzle I gave my students, I am confident that they walked away with something important. First, they did something that archaeologists struggle to achieve: they interpreted a culture that is not clearly known or remembered. Most significantly, they got beyond the pyramids and the bloodletting, the gold and the feathers, to hypothesize about the patterns of thought that motivated the ceremonies, the architecture, and the rituals. This empowered them to take risks in thinking that might not have been possible had answers been more concrete and defined.

Second, students developed a multistep complex project that challenged them to think in terms of organization, structure, process, and persistence toward reaching closure. Too often we never bring things full circle so that students can develop something from the very beginning to the complete end. My students were proud of the thinking they had done, which was reflected in the difficult questions they asked, the skepticism they displayed when someone presented a new theory, and the joy they exhibited when someone said something that was exciting and new. I was proud of the puzzles they created. I know that given the many puzzles that are in their future, they will be less intimidated by the pieces in the box, and they won't hesitate to use the strategies that work best for them to create their own picture of what is possible.

Notes

1. Gardner, H. 1983. *Frames of Mind: The Theory of Multiple Intelligences*. (New York: Basic Books.)
2. This video series is part of an extensive curriculum, "The Second Voyage of the Mimi." 1989. Sunburst Communications.
3. *MayaQuest: The Mystery Trail.* 1995. MECC, 6160 Summit Dr., North Minneapolis, MN.

Response from a Colleague:
Closing the Gap by Beginning
at the End

Chris Hargrave

The whole point of middle school, I think, is to give students the possibility to expand their ways of thinking. Students come to us well-practiced in the face-to-face, concrete world of objects, talk, and activity. We have three years with them to help them develop the kinds of analysis, logic, and systematic questioning that make adolescence and adulthood interesting. But traditionally, we don't really build that bridge; we just assign it. Eighth grade? Okay, time for algebra, primary sources, and research papers. Tammy's chapter has set me to thinking how wrong that approach is.

As middle school teachers, many of us are very good at laying down the first piece of the puzzle—the one we use to touch on our students' personal lives or immediate concerns. Tammy is like the rest of us in that respect. She opens her unit on the Maya by asking students about how they learn and what characterizes their learning. Most of us would use that discussion as a warm-up before launching into a study of the three periods of Mayan civilization, occasionally mentioning the word *learning* when we came to architecture, number systems, or calendar systems. And when we wanted our students to apply all that they had learned by asking them to hypothesize why Mayan urban centers collapsed, we would be disappointed at the flat-footed, commonsense, puzzled responses.

I have done it myself. I remember teaching a unit on early settlements. We discussed the basics of life: food, shelter, even religion and knowledge. We read from the textbook; we looked at some early Neolithic artifacts. As a culminating activity, I asked my students to invent a primitive society, working in groups to create the various aspects of their early civilizations. I expected all kinds of thoughtful extrapolations. What I did get was a mixture of fantasies and commonplace descriptions. I simply had not cut a path from what they knew to what I wanted them to be able to do. I had invited them to write a story, not to engage in anything like archaeology or history. Only as I read their responses did I realize what had happened. Yes, I had engaged them. No, I hadn't educated them. There were no data to work from, no inferences to draw, no way of making judgments about the quality of their reasoning or their final work.

Sobered and wiser, the next year I gave each working group a very specific ecological niche, defining its geography, rainfall, minerals, water supply, and fertility. I gave them the problem of hypothesizing what kind of early civilization might have grown up and flourished there. They had to describe the likely means of survival, one possible form of ritual and religion, and one kind of knowledge or record keeping (such as a number system or calendar). In each case, they had to be able to explain how they reasoned from the ecology to the culture. The results were—if not all the way home—hugely different.

This is exactly the kind of work that Tammy does so well. She has created a carefully built series of observations, discussions, and occasions for building and testing hypotheses. Having reminded her students that they are all learners, she makes the transition to asking them to think about the Maya as learners. She then starts them off with the dot, building on what we had all experienced as learners in the Peabody Museum. She urges her students daily to become increasingly skilled readers of the evidence. The reward for this patient urging begins to surface: a student, struggling to make sense of the complex glyphs on a stela, calls out, "Look at the patterns. The symbols wouldn't keep repeating in different ways if it wasn't letters or numbers!" Gone is the usual division between entry-level connections and more sophisticated inferences. Tammy has effectively built the middle ground that ought to be the discourse of all middle schools.

But as I read on in the chapter, I realized that I was not just reading about an effective middle ground, I was also being taught an important lesson about endpoints. Tammy's invention of the Maya Center at the outset of the unit is a way of forecasting for students where their work is headed. All their research, discussion, arguing, and writing had a point. I could see the effects in Gerrell's essay on what he noticed about the symmetry of Maya design:

> I think that the symmetry the Maya used honored their gods and created a sense of order and pattern . . .

And in Thomas's:

> They were intrapersonal because most things were based on the strong spirit and mental abilities of a person and their [sic] connection with the gods, for example.

As I read these essays I kept thinking that the next time these students think about another civilization, they won't be content to stop at the "stuff" that civilization made, the buildings it built, or the treaties it signed. This is the kind of student thinking that makes you wonder about the possibility of connections across our habitual subject divisions. Might this kind of analysis enable Thomas and Gerrell to examine mathematics problems more carefully? Develop hypotheses? Scrutinize their data in an experiment?

Again, this sent me back to thinking about my own teaching. I, too, would like a classroom of thinkers. But usually I concentrate on the things along the way: Day 1, Day 2 . . . I don't always offer my students such a clear and challenging task to head toward. Often their final task or assessment is something they meet only in the last week. Tammy's Maya Center made me realize how important it is to begin with the end: the final assessment task at which I want my students to succeed. I need to design backwards in order to create a real infrastructure for learning.

There is no closing the gap without beginning at the end.

4

"More of a Questioning Spirit"

Unearthing Ancient Greece

Miriam Nason and Shannon Thomas with the students of Family E and Dennie Palmer Wolf

It is a busy intersection. Only a few blocks away, down at the foot of the hill, a freeway rushes by. The surrounding houses sprout television antennae and telephone wires crisscross the sky. Underfoot the ground is cement and asphalt. There is no question: this is the late twentieth century. So what are those voices doing talking about the dig along the road to Thebes? The trial of Socrates last spring? If, *last spring*, you had been a sixth grader at O'Farrell Community School in San Diego, a member of Family E, and one of the students who goes flying back and forth between Room 115 and Room 107, you would have known how to live in both contemporary San Diego and fifth-century Greece. Before eight and after three you would have been one of the 1,500 sixth, seventh, and eighth graders rushing from locker to classroom, talking to your friends in Spanish or Tagalog, or studying for a math test. But between the first and the last bell your address would have been Dig 2, Quadrant 3, along the road that winds its way between Athens and Thebes. Or perhaps you would be inside the courtroom where the jurors solemnly cast their lots into the jar to determine whether Socrates lives or dies. Or maybe you wrote a four-stanza poem with Homer in mind, or were amazed that Pythagoras could have seen so much in just a triangle.

Like many other urban middle schools, O'Farrell's job is to see that all, not just a few, students reach the high standards that we all hear so much about. We, like our colleagues in Los Angeles or Kansas City, use the tools of interdisciplinary teaching, heterogeneous grouping, and portfolios to engage our students in doing high-quality work that honors, rather than homogenizes, the variety in their histories and cultural backgrounds. In addition, we have organized ourselves into educational families where teams of three teachers work intensively with the same group of seventy-five students in order to create ongoing expectations and supports.

As in countless other middle schools, we teach world history and cultures in the sixth grade. Like many other teachers, we have taken the forced march across sixty civilizations in eight months and turned it into exploration of a few chosen civilizations, and we have melded together our work in history, geography, literature, and sometimes mathematics and science. All this we have done for a reason that sounds almost simpleminded: we want our students to understand, not vaguely remember, the civilizations they study.

One of those major explorations is of ancient Greece. In a world that has grown very divided about whose history and civilization should be taught, and tense about how often Western civilization edges others to the margin, it is important to say why, as teachers of students who are largely Filipino, African-American, Asian, and Latino, we feel strongly about dedicating such a large portion of our teaching to what happened in the fourth and fifth centuries in Greece. It is not that Greek culture is the only great civilization, or the best one, or the only one we look to for the roots of our own civilization. Two other reasons compel us. The first is something one of our students said as clearly as we ever could:

> The myths and things are like our backside, we don't talk
> about them all the time now, we just worry about hairstyles
> and new clothes, but somewhere in your mind there is
> always one little spark that is mythology.

He is right. Much of what the Greeks left us—the legends, the elements of science, and the ideas of democracy—are at our "backside." Own them and you can enter many conversations that matter: those of researchers, writers, jurors, and judges.

But it is the second reason that we want to explore in this chapter. At the center of our study of the Greeks are some of the most fundamental questions that human beings should be able to take on: What do you know? How do you know it? What is the evidence? Why do you trust it? What questions are still unanswered? When do you know enough to choose or judge or decide? Most history texts tell students that the Greeks were great thinkers— people who thought their way to philosophy, geometry, and science. But from another perspective, what Greek civilization really left behind was the habit and art of asking questions, along with the high standards of expecting good answers.

Both of us come by this interest in questions honestly. Growing up, both of us were blessed: no one ever told us to stop pestering them with questions. Just the opposite. Now, as colleagues, we teach in a school designed from the ground up by its faculty. Like all good inventors, as a faculty we suffer from the "I bet it could be done better" itch. On days when there is time, we constantly ask one another, "How do you know that works with kids? What's the evidence?" And in a school where graduation from eighth grade is based on the quality of work in students' portfolios, we are constantly asking students, "What's evidence that you have met the standards?"

Our pact is that if we are going to study ancient Greece, we have to create a culture built upon raising and answering good questions. But that is something akin to teaching a language; it demands immersion in a world where everything is up for examination and where there is no stepping outside the web of connections and echoes. Both history and literature have to point in the same direction, and math and science have to join in. The questions raised in Mrs. Nason's Room must be live material down the corridor in Mr. Thomas's Room. In essence, we have to build parallel laboratories for going after the truth, or at least understanding.

The First Question: How Do You Write This Chapter for Twenty-five Voices?

This chapter is itself a case in point. How would we write it in a way that would reflect all of the different perspectives? By the time we followed through with those questions, we had invented our way toward a very different approach. To begin, we wrote a short outline of what we did in class. PACE researchers worked with us, creating detailed transcripts of classroom interactions and interviews with students. We collected and shared samples of student work, discussing them with other teachers in the network. Through that collaboration, we generated a first draft manuscript. When PACE returned it to us, it was peppered with questions for us and for our former students. Using our work together and those questions as the core texts, we invited students we had worked with during the previous two years (now seventh and eighth graders) to join us for a Socratic seminar on what they had learned with us.

The questions from PACE were not simple. For instance, they asked students:

> Do you ever find yourself making connections back to what you learned in your study of the Greeks? Maybe, when you watch the news, read the newspaper, or read in your history books?

But students answered and discussed the issues with startling clarity, precision, and feeling:

> In the Trojan War, we would have discussions about how different it was for the soldiers and the people back at home. It took Odysseus ten years to get back home and when he got there there were suitors after his wife and everything was changed. A modern day example is in Bosnia (where the war dragged on). It must be completely different for the soldiers and the children and families in Bosnia.

We joined in, too. As soon as students started talking about the myths they remembered, Mr. Thomas asked:

> When we were studying myths, do you remember how we approached the question of whether or not they were true?

They did:

When we would argue with Mr. Thomas about if the myths were true, we would say, "Well, we found this artifact, or this about Troy, or this burial site. And then we'd go into Mr. Thomas's class and we'd use [what we'd learned] in Mrs. Nason's room to talk to Mr. Thomas. I liked that then Mr. Thomas would ask us very intruding questions and we'd have to search over our minds.

The result is that the "we" in this chapter is a shape-shifter, like the Greek god, Proteus. Sometimes it is Mrs. Nason and Mr. Thomas speaking as colleagues, sometimes it is the seventh and eighth graders who all think of themselves as graduates of the dig, and sometimes it is researchers and teachers who have had an unusual chance to collaborate.

Creating a Culture of Questioning: How Do You Set Up to Dig Deep?

For eight weeks, Room 115 became a combination of a research center and an archaeological dig. With a number of other school sites, we field-tested "Archaeotype," a computer simulation of an excavation along the road between Athens and Thebes. In the simulation, students could scan their quadrant of the site to locate buried artifacts. Once located, they could excavate and transport the artifacts to an electronic laboratory. Inside the lab, the pedestal or shield or coin could be weighed, measured, rotated, and enlarged. Then the detective work began. It was up to students to use the program's CD-ROM library of images and descriptions, as well as our own classroom resources, to identify what they had unearthed. This is where questioning had to become the tool of choice. Just like practicing archaeologists, students frequently had only fragments to work with. Important clues were often broken off or obscured with wear. As at any site where people dwell over centuries and where rivers change their course and frost heaves the ground, artifacts from different periods can be deceptively similar. So each find had to be examined and evaluated carefully in its own right.

This work with Archaeotype could easily have turned into a guess-and-check treasure hunt to see who could locate the most artifacts the quickest—except that we situated the dig at the center of a much broader investigation of Greek civilization. Three core classes of twenty-five students each rotated through the excavation daily, working in hundred-minute blocks of time that allowed them to conduct research and participate in the extensive analysis that would be critical to their work as archaeologists. Each class was to become experts in a specific time period: Class 1 took on the earliest forms of Greek civilization, from 2000 to 1400 B.C.; Class 2 was in charge of the Bronze Age and the Dark Age, from 1400 to 800 B.C.; and Class 3 was responsible for the years 800 to 200 B.C., the Archaic, Classical, and Hellenistic periods. Students worked in four teams, one for each quadrant of the site. Each team was responsible for every artifact found. For each artifact they discovered, students report based on a set of guide questions that they had created. These questions ranged from the factual ("Where was this artifact found?") to ones that demanded research, analysis, and interpretation ("What evidence did you use in identifying this object?" or "What do we have today that is like this artifact?").

The reports, though brief, were challenging for students to produce. It was easy enough to weigh and measure, and not so hard to hazard a guess about what the artifact could be. But laying out a hypothesis, incorporating a probable identification backed up by corroborating evidence, was frankly hard. Going from the probable identification and use to what that revealed (or might reveal) about Greek civilization was perhaps even more difficult. A lab report on a marble inscription makes this clear. (See Figure 4–1.) The students had studied the physical appearance of the object closely and were clear about its distinctive features: "the nose of the artifact is leveled with the eyes." However, when students tried to identify it—which demanded the synthesis, rather than listing, of important features; inference; and the use of outside sources—they struggled:

> We really couldn't figure out what kind of people created it, but we think it is really old. The artifact was used to put on your face for entertainment. From my opinion, I think that it

FIGURE 4–1.

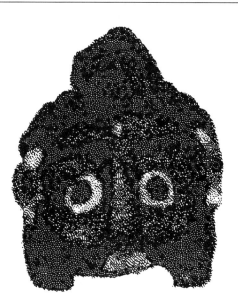

This artifact is a mask . It weight is 25 grams. The height of it is 7 cm. and the width is 7 c.m.. The color of the mask is gold yellow black and red. It is made out of glass. The mask has big eyes and the outline of the face looks as if there were pieces missing . The nose of this artifact is leveled with the eyes. The mouth of the mask is very large. The condition is fair but if the pieces were there then it would look a little better . We really couldn't figure out what kind of people created it but we think it is really old . The artifact was used to put on your face for intertanment. From my opinion I think that it is from when homer the writer was around because at that time theater and acting was very popular. We could learn from this how there culture was and how they had thier own kind of intertanment. I think that this artifact is similar to ours know days because we still wear masks for intertanment too!

is from when Homer the writer was around because at that time theater and acting was very popular.

Since this kind of gathering of clues into a plausible pattern was the heart of what we were trying to do, it was very important for the teachers to respond to the reports carefully in a one-on-one exchange with the teams, posing questions and pulling for the evidence, providing students with specific information with which to revise. We worked on a four-point system that ran from beginning (1), to developing (2), to accomplished (3), to exemplary (4). Even though this team's lab report was lengthy, its lack of clarity and the thin quality of the evidence led to a rating of 1.5.

Even once students had the hang of researching their hunches and backing them up, the work of drawing inferences still presented a stiff challenge. In Figure 4–3, for instance, a team of students has done a fine job of identifying an object and researching its use. They have even been careful to define the specialty terms they uncover (e.g., *hoplite*) rather than simply copying them blindly. Still, digging out what the artifact teaches them about Greek civilization is hard. They can write, "We know that it was used to do battle. We feel that the Greeks were very intelligent because of the design of the sword." But exactly what is it about the sword that makes it proof of intelligence at work? Is it the shape of the handle that made it easy to hold on to in the heat of battle? Is it the smelting of several different kinds of metals? Is it that the design was borrowed from neighboring cultures? And just what does this sword tell us about Greek society? That war was an integral part of it? That infantrymen were valuable enough to be well armed?

If we were going to make substantial headway in using evidence and drawing interesting and supportable conclusions, we had to invent classroom exchanges that would promote discussion, challenge, and revision. We realized, however, that since many of our students possessed little sense of history, outside of that represented by their own families,' and since few of them have had much experience researching other cultures, we had to build a rich and reliable fund of information that was available to everyone. So

FIGURE 4–2.

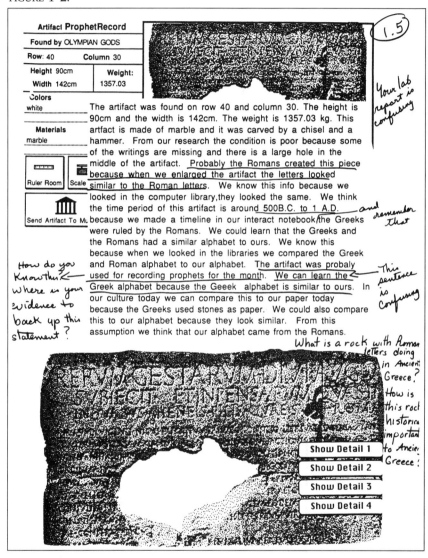

FIGURE 4–3.

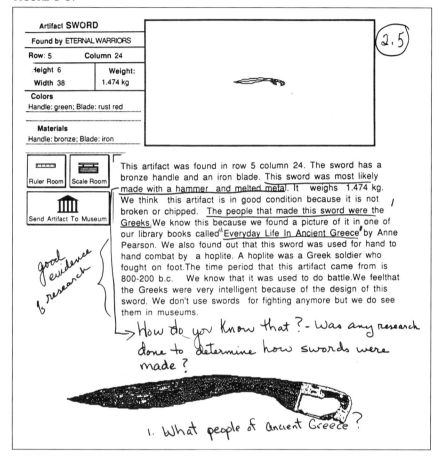

we jointly produced an enormous public time line on which we plotted our growing knowledge of Greek civilizations. Each team within a class was to become expert in specific aspects of Greek culture. For example, Team A was in charge of literature, science, philosophy, and religion; Team C took charge of government, economy, money, and laws. Each team chose a "crew chief" who acted as a facilitator for the group, directing discussions, settling disputes, and creating work schedules that guaranteed fair access to the materials in the classroom library and the three computers we shared. Each crew maintained for its lab reports, notes, observations, and reflections a notebook that other students could request to see. They were also responsible for printing an enlarged copy of their artifact to post on a graph of the site for all crews and classes to see. If student work is any proof, then this groundwork was successful. Two students (S1 and S2) make this plain as they explain how much their overall sense of Greek sculpture informed their work:

S1: We found a statue, well, at first we didn't know. It turned out to be a warrior king. Our first hunch was that it was just one of their gods. At first, we couldn't tell whether it was Roman or Greek, or what time period. But the early statues were not full of life—lifelike.

S2: They were firm and rigid. It was not until later that they got the technology to make them off-balance, like standing on one foot. There were three Greek periods. The third was really lifelike. Smooth and graceful. It was hard to be sure because the Romans copies, so it was the exact same way. We were just doing a random search by that time and we found a picture of an arm in a book. And we shouted out, "There it is, there it is."

Twice a week, we held a class discussion, designed to help students push their understanding of hypotheses, evidence, and inference. We focused our attention on three core processes. First, we shared recent discoveries across the different quadrants of the excavation quads. We used these to build theories about Greek civilization in each of the time periods. Second, students acted as peer reviewers. It was their duty to raise questions and to draw connections between the information that was building up in different quadrants. Finally, students evaluated how they were working as a group, both socially and intellectually.

Gradually, students came to hold themselves to an increasingly high standard of performance on their lab reports. The net result of this searching, testing out of possibilities, challenging, and elaborating on one another's work was that students' lab reports became not simply more detailed, or more accurate. They also became both more responsible ("How do I know what I am claiming is, or could be, true?") and more thought-provoking ("Have I really taken this information as far as I can?) Figure 4–4 offers an example.

It is best to let students have the last word about our work with Archaeotype. They say it with authority:

> The important part was that you had to do research. You had to know enough. Our [artifact] was part of a building. But it was upside down. So we had to rotate it. So the main theme here is you've got to research, go in and out, turn it around in your mind, to become successful as an archaeologist.

A Seminar for Young Philosophers

Several rooms away, in 107, we took the mind as the site for our excavations. We began by reading the myths that answer the most basic of human questions, "How did the world begin?" and "How was it that the human race appeared on the face of the earth?" We looked at how the Greeks, and other peoples, answered in their myths large questions about the origin of the world, the source of good and evil, and the origin of fire. Students wrote their own myths about questions they believed an early civilization would have wanted answers to. The point was that we were not writing stories so much as positing how central the habit of asking questions is to being human. Thinking aloud about this, even a year later, one student, who could still remember Prometheus, Persephone, and the Titans, explained:

> The myths were any people's way of explaining how things came to be, how they could change, how there could be mortals and immortals.
>
> The Greeks were very intellectual people. They argued a lot and did a lot of serious thinking and that doesn't happen too often these days. One of the biggest things is the rush in life, radios and TV. Now people only think about the little things, not about the whole perspective and the whole world. The Greeks had nothing else to do so they would gather to talk about the meaning of life. That wasn't until the end. First

FIGURE 4–4.

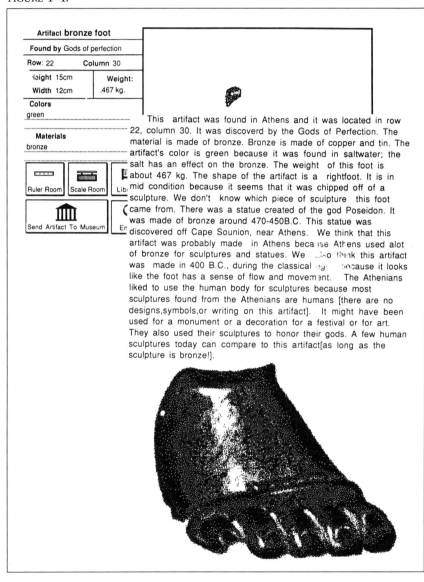

Artifact bronze foot	
Found by Gods of perfection	
Row: 22	**Column** 30
‹eight 15cm	**Weight:**
Width 12cm	.467 kg.
Colors	
green	
Materials	
bronze	

Ruler Room | Scale Room | Lib‹

Send Artifact To Museum | En

This artifact was found in Athens and it was located in row 22, column 30. It was discoverd by the Gods of Perfection. The material is made of bronze. Bronze is made of copper and tin. The artifact's color is green because it was found in saltwater; the salt has an effect on the bronze. The weight of this foot is about 467 kg. The shape of the artifact is a rightfoot. It is in mid condition because it seems that it was chipped off of a sculpture. We don't know which piece of sculpture this foot came from. There was a statue created of the god Poseidon. It was made of bronze around 470-450B.C. This statue was discovered off Cape Sounion, near Athens. We think that this artifact was probably made in Athens beca.se Athens used alot of bronze for sculptures and statues. We ...so think this artifact was made in 400 B.C., during the classical ·g· ·ecause it looks like the foot has a sense of flow and movem∍nt. The Athenians liked to use the human body for sculptures because most sculptures found from the Athenians are humans [there are no designs,symbols,or writing on this artifact]. It might have been used for a monument or a decoration for a festival or for art. They also used their sculptures to honor their gods. A few human sculptures today can compare to this artifact[as long as the sculpture is bronze!].

they made myths and told stories, but that's the way they thought about life, using their myths.

At the same time, students were also starting to think about what it means to offer an explanation. We set this off by asking them if the Greek myths were true. Already they were beginning to knit together our discussions and what they were learning in their excavations. As one student remembers it:

> When we would argue with Mr. Thomas about if the myths were true, we would say, "Well, we found this artifact, or this about Troy, or this burial site." And then we'd go into Mr. Thomas's class and we'd use what we'd done in Mrs. Nason's room to talk to Mr. Thomas. I liked that Mr. Thomas would ask very intruding questions and we'd have to search over our minds.

Another student points out how sophisticated those discussions became about the limits of our knowledge:

> I'd like to add the ways that we worked on whether something was true or not was we would go to see if it was more like something we have today or if we have it nowadays in our history of the Greeks. But I think only a few of us went into the possibility of something being in a myth that we *didn't* know about. Something that the Greeks had that we didn't know. All we did basically was to try to determine whether a myth was true based on what we have today.

With the myths behind us, we moved on to reading Homer's *Odyssey*. For each chapter, different students took responsibility for summarizing what had happened. The mixture of myth and history was an ideal proving ground for sharpening our discussion of what could count as true. It led to long discussions of whether we could believe that Troy or Odysseus existed, just because archaeologists had unearthed a walled city with carvings of heroic figures and *called* those figures by the names in Homer's texts. This discussion captured the imagination of many students, since, as young urban citizens, they are keenly aware that official history, whether it involves television, the newspaper, or textbooks, does not always reflect everyone's experience accurately or equally. Months later, during the course of a portfolio interview, a student explained why he couldn't use *The Iliad* as a reliable source in helping him to identify an artifact at his dig site:

> It is like Socrates. Before he announced that there were no gods, he would say, "Prove it." He would say, "Don't give me a scroll with a myth on it, or a gift that a god gave you. Give me proof." And he would question and question to see if he could get an answer that he believed in. Just because you find it mentioned in a book that *says* it is history, doesn't mean it is.

We spoke about the transition from mythology and narrative as explanation to philosophy and proof. We discussed the different pre-Socratic philosophers and their efforts to build theories that would explain the origins and composition of the universe.

> They had lots of different answers about how the earth was made. One philosopher thought it was with a number system, he had one for male, and two for female, and on like that. Another one had it made of the four elements: earth, air, fire, and water. And another one thought it was made from atoms. That a civilization that far back thought about all those things. We only have better technology to do the investigating, that's all.
>
> Their main thing was, is this fact true, is that not true, more of a what about this, what about that. They were constantly questioning life. The main thing about philosophy was about truth.

As the closing part of our work together, we looked at Socrates as a teacher of young people. We talked about the kinds of questions he taught his students to ask—and how his method of frank, persistent questioning can be experienced as disrespectful and can even become dangerous. We read about the trial of Socrates and the students reenacted it, taking up both sides of the argument.

Mr. Thomas he had us in a Socratic seminar, Mr. Thomas would be Socrates and we would be the young people learning. And he would question us about every thing. He would ask someone a question but it would sometimes go round in a circle, "Why?" "Because I think it is this way." "Why?" "Because I think this way." But Mr. Thomas didn't give up. It was fun. I really miss those times.

We also had, like a conversation, a debate between Socrates and Homer and it was that we would question each other and expect answers and then add something on to it, if they would give us a good enough answer.

An Afterword

We were lucky. Our method of raising and answering questions was deliberately echoed in students' math and science classes. For example, in their math classes, students experimented with the Pythagorean theorem, measuring triangle after triangle in order to rediscover the regularities that Pythagoras first saw fifteen hundred years ago. They returned to basic Greek experiments, such as rubbing wool with amber to "make feathers dance," that is, to create static electricity.

But no matter how rich a mixture you intend to prepare, you never really know what will sink in. You can't predict whether a student will remember the principles you meant to teach about the trial of Socrates, or an argument she had with the kid sitting next to her about who would cast the first vote, or whether to open the window. However, during the seminar with seventh and eighth graders two years later, we are amazed at what they have retained:

Socrates questioned many aspects of life and he was just on trial for that, but I believe that he was really trying to honor man's intelligences and tell them that the gods are not their masters, but they can take responsibility, they don't need to believe in the importance of the gods. He questioned many aspects because he believed that it was important to know as much as possible. He was not afraid of the unknown. He had

students and they grew up to be the great men of Greece.
People were angry because they couldn't answer his
questions. He had to stop teaching or die? He wouldn't stop
teaching, he just drank the hemlock and lay down and died.
He is a great man because if he didn't do what he did, the
world would be a land of primitives. We wouldn't be as
smart or capable of completing our mission in life.

Personally, I think that Socrates was like a key that fit in a
lock and he opened up how we think. And I really admire
him.

By now, it is long past afternoon—after five, in fact. The pizza is
eaten, the juice and soda are gone. Mrs. Nason tries to end the seminar on Archaeotype and Greek thought at least several times. But
it's not so easy; there is a kind of drive to make closing comments:

It was the first civilization to honor man's intelligences, it
was the first civilization not to depend on gods and
goddesses. Man was more powerful than gods. They can
make their own decisions. We have much greater technology,
but we have to take a moment to appreciate how much they
could already do.

If more of civilizations nowadays had Socrates or other
philosophers, it would be different. Now people just take
their stuff and learn it and that's it. If we were more like the
Greeks we would have more of a questioning spirit, I mean,
why is two and two four, why couldn't it be something else?

Truth is their religion. Truth, knowledge, and justice. It was
for their own future. When Rome came along, they
conquered a very good civilization. Now it is just a place
where people go to forget their troubles. It's because as
people we worship technology. But without knowledge you
have nothing.

Mrs. Nason refers back to a moment earlier in the afternoon, when
two students suddenly realized that the artifacts they dug up and
investigated two years ago are actually fragments of the same
large inscription. They had leaned forward, pieced the fragments

together, and examined the fit of the letters. There was a moment of hubbub as the thrill of discovery took over once again. Remembering that moment, Mrs. Nason's voice, though soft, carries:

> You know, Mr. Thomas and I talked about how we had to improve that kind of sharing. We might have made that connection last year if we'd been able to figure out how to make that happen. You see, as teachers, we are still learning.

The chairs scrape. Jackets come out. The seminar ends.
A good number of "questioning spirits" head out into the air and the new evening.

Response from a Colleague

Dennie Palmer Wolf

When I interview, I set the same challenge each time. I try to listen to the current of thought running through what the speaker is saying so closely that when a pause comes, I can ask a question that fishes the deep pools. That question is at once evidence that I have listened and just enough of a stretch so that, if the speaker will "go for it," an answer luminous with intent, concentration, and thought breaks the surface. I want to hear mind, heart, and imagination humming, on the spot. As work, this kind of questioning is a cross between bird-watching, throwing a perfectly centered pot, and turning up a treasure in a secondhand book store. Done right, it leaves you physically tired although you never stirred. And, when it works—for both speaker and interviewer—you believe again in the possibility of words as open-handed gestures, rather than coins, tickets—or aimless small BBs.

It is now almost three years since I first practiced this challenge in a lounge just beyond Miriam Nason's and Shannon Thomas's rooms at O'Farrell Community School. It was at the end of the first year of the Archaeotype project and a sixth grader was explaining the simulation to me. As I listened and took notes, the question came to me:

> You've been learning how to make sense of a civilization
> from its artifacts. Suppose, a century from now, someone
> found this laptop computer, what do you think they could
> tell from it about our civilization?

Undaunted, the student waded in, as careful as any archaeologist walking a new site for the first time:

S: Would this person be able to turn it on? Would it still work?
I: Let's say they could figure out a way.
S: Would the files still be on it?
I: Yes, imagine the files were there.
S: Would this file of you and me talking be there?
I: Yes.
S: Well, I think if they read the files—if they knew our language—they could tell a lot about schools, well, no, about *this* school. They wouldn't know that it is different from a lot of other schools.
I: What could they tell?
S: That the adults thought the kids could think.
I: What would be the evidence?
S: That kids were doing the investigations. And being asked to come to the conclusions . . . and that adults bothered to ask them what they thought, like now.

A half hour later, I spoke to another student. He was fascinated by the fact that the class was field-testing the program and making recommendations about how the designers might change it. As he explained to me about "beta-testing Archaeotype," another question came to me:

> So imagine that it is four weeks from now, and you are writing a letter with your recommendations to the designers. Can you dictate it to me?

This student also waded in.

> I have two things to recommend. First, the artifacts shouldn't be all jumbled together, so you can find a very early statue right next to a Roman coin. It should be more like a real dig is. You should be able to get clues about your artifact from where you find it, from the kind of building you think it is in, from the kind of neighborhood the building is in. And there is a second thing. When you go to put the artifacts in the museum, right now you can just sort of store them along with the lab reports. It would make much more sense, it would be much better, if it was all four teams' job to try to

reconstruct the city that was once there. Then you would really have to make use of the research that you did and it would have to work with what other people did. For instance, like in my class, I would have found out that I had part of a stone tablet that someone else had another part of and we would have had to put our finds together. And then we would have had to figure out what kind of a building that tablet would have been in, from what else was around, what kind of neighborhood. And from that we could begin to tell something about the kind of life the Greeks were living in that part of the city. It would be much more like what I think real archaeologists try to do. I think they made it too simple for kids in the end. We could do that."

Several years later, I once again began to hang out regularly in and around Rooms 107 and 115. It was like fishing for trout in a place where the water is deep and cool. It was full of big, wise fish. One day, I sat down by two of the current crop of young archaeologists, Keith and André, and asked them to explain to me what made the excavations and research challenging:

KEITH: We named our team "The Gods of Perfection." But it didn't exactly turn out that way. This bronze foot misled us for four weeks. It was green, bronze turns that outside, so we began to think that it was part of a statue. [He explains how sponge divers have uncovered antique statues off the Greek coastline.] So we were imagining that it might have been transported and then the ship sank. We hunted for statues in all kind of books. We were just looking at bronze statues and on the statues there were some missing feet, so we just tried to put them together.

INTERVIEWER: What gave you a clue that you might not be right?

ANDRÉ: Well, Mrs. Nason had told us if we would research a little more, we would find a clue, so we went searching through the computer library and there was a bronze foot guard.

KEITH: Bronze foot guards were used by warriors, by Spartan warriors, when they go to war, but all they found was that some of the warriors wore them, like the rich people wore them.

ANDRÉ: So it comes up between the toes and then it has this latch thing. . . .

KEITH: Hinge . . . for the toes so for it to be easier for them to move around.

INTERVIEWER: So that tells you they had foot guards, but what does it tell you about war in Sparta?

KEITH: I think in Sparta, they usually used bronze for armor and weapons and things like that. But we are not sure about that. We think it is that bronze was like strong and you could reuse it. So I think that they liked the idea of making these things from bronze, because if one piece of armor was to get messed up, all they could do was just to melt it down again and reuse it.

INTERVIEWER: But what else do you learn about Sparta from the foot guards?

ANDRÉ: Well, some people wore them and other people didn't. That tells you something about the Spartan army right there. They gave each warrior like different kinds of ranks. In our research books, it shows that there is an archer and they are like usually creeping [??] and then there are the hoplites that wear the foot guard and they wear, um, all the important armor.

INTERVIEWER: Why did they get such important armor?

KEITH: Because they are more skilled. They are like worth protecting more. And the reason why they have the bronze outfit for the warriors, is to come out more, to be open, because in the other wars, the other side that fought them, had almost the same thing, but the Spartans had bronze, and the others, well maybe, they had gold or silver, and so the Spartans could like follow who was with them.

INTERVIEWER: So like a uniform for a team? . . . So what can you tell about the technology that the Greeks had way back then?

KEITH: I would say that they were pretty advanced. I think their shields would be like our bulletproof vests. I think that our gloves would be their hand guards. 'Cause most of the time, when they fight, the warriors will usually go for their wrist or their neck. Because that is one way to make them die easily, because you bleed faster from those parts of your body.

INTERVIEWER: So the foot guards and the hand guards helped to protect them?

KEITH: Yes, um, they have armor and most of the time their armor was kind of high. I would also say from the footguard that the Greeks didn't like to be hurt. They would put on just about any type of armor to protect themselves. To survive.

KEITH: Different kinds of warriors had different kinds of armor. The archers they wore leather and they did not have armored hats. They had pointed hats like elves. I guess they didn't think the archers were worth all that much, they were sort of like slaves.

Usually a class leaves only certain kinds of artifacts in its wake: notes on the chapter, colored maps, unit tests. Here was quite different evidence. And, if the evidence was right, Archaeotype, paired with the trial of Socrates and the rediscovery of Pythagoras and static electricity, left quite a different trail. Yes, there were notes on ancient Greece, and maps, and answers to the questions raised in the lab reports. But there was also more: a zeal for finding out and a humility about being certain.

Epilogue

But I Don't Teach the Maya . . .

Julie Craven

Archaeology and the Maya. What do these topics have to offer me? I teach humanities to seventh and eighth graders in Cambridge, Massachusetts, on a two-year curriculum cycle that alternates between China and the Middle East during one year, and U.S. History from the Civil War to World War II during the other. Common sense would dictate that I spend what precious nonteaching time I have on reading, conversation, or workshops directly related to what I teach. And common sense is right to a point.

But teachers don't just transmit curriculum, they create it. And what they create is uniquely shaped by the needs and personalities of the students and communities at hand, so no workshop will ever offer exactly what any one teacher needs. In this world, I am better served by a well-structured experience that challenges me to learn and reflect than by an experience of exactly matched content. Thus, the professional development described in these pages—with Bill Saturno and the Maya—has everything to do with me.

My experience as a curriculum seminar codeveloper, particularly in the Maya seminar, expanded my ideas on how to frame curriculum units. The biggest challenge for me over the years has not been gathering information about the topics I am to teach. There are always more than enough resources and activity guides—anyone who has planned to teach China, the Middle East, or the civil rights movement will concur. In fact, I am often overwhelmed by the volume and range of information on any topic, and I am an adult with years of practice making sense of large chunks of information. My students, however, don't have this experience, so I need to find the unifying thread for them. If I am planning to introduce my students to a long stretch of history or to another culture, how will I connect the pieces of the puzzle so that they become part of a single image my students can ponder and appreciate? Moreover, how do I even get them to want to gather all the pieces in the first place? This is what I want any readings or conversations about teaching to address. And I have high standards; I want to test-drive before I buy. I want to go through models of how to approach these intimidating topics as a learner first. Give me a thread I can believe in, and from there I can deconstruct and build. In this light, the time I spent exploring the Maya has made all the difference.

Helping to bring the curriculum seminar on the Maya to life gave me firsthand experience with the power of archaeology as a driving force for gathering and making sense of information. As both codeveloper of and participant in the seminar on the Maya, I pondered the meaning of a series of dots and dashes laid out before me; once I knew they were the Mayan number system, I searched reproductions of Mayan stelae for numbers and other symbols and dared to form hypotheses about the purpose behind these monuments. After learning more about the rudiments of Mayan civilization, I could distinguish patterns and clues in what had once been only attractive slides of ancient architectural remains.

By the end of the first day, my colleagues and I bent our visiting archaeologist's ear with our theories and questions, then nodded our appreciation and awe as he shared information and directed our attention to keener observations that led us ever deeper into new theories and understandings. We looked at the murals of Bonampak and didn't just observe that there were blood sacrifices depicted within; we wanted to explore the relationship of the sacrifice to the land, with its seasonal cycles, and the connection of all this to the Mayan creation story, the *Popul Vuh*. We only stopped our theorizing when the museum pushed us out at closing time.

On the second day of the curriculum seminar, we deconstructed the experience we had so enjoyed to try to pinpoint what it was that had engaged us. We identified four elements: an entry point that was accessible to all and established the need (and desire) to know more (the dots and dashes that had intrigued us also made sense to us—we all used number systems); the primary documents and artifacts that allowed us to be "on site" as thinkers; the secondary sources and knowledgeable human resources to test our theories and build new understandings and questions; and a structure that balanced our time between primary and secondary sources so that our theories stayed closer to scientific hypotheses than wild guesses. Our curiosity was never overpowered by frustration over not really knowing. We were no different than our students: at some moment in struggling to puzzle out a mystery we, too, called out, "Just tell us."

At the end of the first phase of the seminar, my job changed. I became the teacher-researcher who supported other teacher-participants in developing their own units on the Maya, some of which appear in this volume. Yet a year later, back in the classroom myself, the thrill I experienced exploring the Maya still excites me. Reproducing that thrill for my students has become the focal point of any curriculum I design. I am determined to create experiences where my students start their own journeys of discovery in which they see the focus of their exploration unfold into emerging, yet comprehensible, complexity. So, in the year I taught U.S. History, we approached Reconstruction by starting at the civil rights movement, a movement with which all students had some familiarity. Students first looked at a video that chronicled the chain of events leading up to the Voting Rights Act of 1964. They were dismayed. None of them could let go of the question of why this act was needed when African Americans had been freed 100 years before. They wanted to figure out what had happened, so we pored over primary source documents. We spent days with the thirteenth, fourteenth, and fifteenth Amendments; black codes and sharecropper contracts; and speeches by Frederick Douglass, W. E. B. DuBois, and Ida B. Wells.[1] Just as I had developed an appreciation of the Maya as a complex civilization with a vibrant past, my students grew to see the civil rights movement as one point in a complex chain of events and individual actions that went back as far as they wanted to look.

With that experience behind me, I entered the second year of my curriculum cycle. As I prepared to teach a unit on China, I kept thinking of how I had entered Mayan culture by following a trail of dots and dashes that had led me into wanting to know more. That these symbols were the Mayan number system was not insignificant to their appeal: I, too, used a number system, and I was unavoidably drawn into noticing where our systems were similar and where they differed. That realization had made me wonder how else we were alike. So I began asking myself what comparable entry point I could give my students for studying China. We ended up looking at the meaning of certain Chinese characters. I started with 女 and asked them what they thought it meant (woman). I made sure they had reasons for their guesses. That was fun but quick. Then I gave them a series of compound characters that incorporated the character for woman, and asked them for more supported hypotheses. When the character for woman 女 is combined with a symbol indicating a roof 宀 so that it is 安, what could it mean? (peace.) What about when it is combined with the character for child 子 to become 好 (good). I moved on: what might this character mean 家, if you know that it is a combination of the symbol for roof 宀 and the character for pig 豕? (family.) So, what does it mean to have woman next to family 嫁? (Marriage, in which the woman goes to the house of the man.)[2] Neither language nor attitudes toward women and ideas about families are unique to China, and as we discussed our guesses and our reasons behind the characters, the students kept pointing out similarities and differences not just with their own culture, but with many others they knew about. They also had many questions about Chinese beliefs, and were impressively cautious about claiming that they could know what Chinese believe just from looking at a few characters. In short, they had entered their study of China.

From there our study unfolded into an exploration of the primary texts of three important Chinese belief systems: the *Tao Te Ching* for Taoism, the *Analects* for Confucianism, and the *Pali Canon* for Buddhism.[3] We took a trip to the Museum of Fine Arts to examine representations of Buddhas over time. Reading *The Joy Luck Club* by Amy Tan[4] let us bridge the worlds of beliefs, history, and personal experiences; we ended with research into contemporary Chinese history that the students had to incorporate into a believable dialogue between two characters in *The Joy Luck Club*. In the dialogues, I saw what I had hoped for: evidence of an appreciation for China's complex culture. My students interpreted events using the values of Chinese belief systems, pulled in Chinese sayings they had uncovered in *The Joy Luck Club*, and had their characters recognize connections between the historic event they were discussing and more current events in U.S. history that they might have experienced directly. The following is an excerpt from a short skit that two students, Sydaiya Gadson-Williams and Kate Dudgeon, wrote comparing the Tiananmen Square demonstration in China to the civil rights movement.

Act I

Guangzhou, China—1990. The home of AIYI and LILI, JING-MEI WOO'S sisters. JING-MEI is looking at a Chinese newspaper and sees that everyone writes favorably about the government. No one writes critically about the government like in American newspapers. It seems to her that the people have no freedom of speech.

JING-MEI: What's up with this paper? Why don't people write anything critical about the government in the newspaper?

AIYI: Well, people don't have freedom of speech in China like in America. So people can't say anything bad about the government.

JING-MEI: Has anyone done anything about it?

AIYI: Actually, a group of college students from thirty different universities protested in 1989.

JING-MEI: Oh ya, I remember when that happened. The Tiananmen Square demonstration. Our government was very upset, especially because they had worked so hard to

make relations better between our countries. We saw some
on TV and read about it in the newspapers. Tell me more
about it. What was it like to be in the same country when it
was happening? It must have been scary.

AIYI: You're right. It was pretty scary. Lots of people died
during this time. It happened about 6 months ago, and it
was the biggest demonstration ever in China.

JING-MEI: But wait a minute. I don't really understand. What
started it?

AIYI: The Tiananmen Square demonstration. Everything
political that happens in China seems to happen in
Tiananmen Square. The square is huge, right in the middle
of Beijing. It has been the center of Chinese politics for
more than three centuries. It's where Mao Ze Dong
proclaimed the beginning of the People's Republic of
China and where mourners of Zhou Enlai clashed with
police. The mourners were those who criticized political
people closest to Mao. They called it the "Tiananmen
Incident." People here want the same things that people
everywhere want. We want freedom of choice and a
chance to prosper. We don't have that in China like in
America.

JING-MEI: What choices exactly?

AIYI: It isn't any one choice. It is just choice in general.
Like in America, you can choose to have an abortion or
not to have an abortion. Or you can choose to be gay,
and have freedom of speech. See, here in China, the
government makes all the decisions for everyone. We
have no say.

JING-MEI: You know, there was a protest similar to this one in
America about thirty, forty years ago.

AIYI: Really? What was it?

JING-MEI: It was the Civil Rights Movement.

AIYI: What were they protesting for?

JING-MEI: They were protesting for whites and blacks to have
equal rights.

AIYI: But how was it similar to the Tiananmen Square
  demonstration?
JING-MEI: It was similar because the government made the
  choice that they didn't have equal rights and they were
  protesting so that they could make the decision to be
  segregated or not.

Throughout the course of our study of China, we kept building
theories and coming back to previously identified questions, so
that by the end of the unit, their notebooks were more dog-eared
than I had ever seen. We hadn't dug up artifacts, but we had been
archaeologists, according to Bill Saturno's broader definition—and
we'd had fun.

My quest for entry points continues. My teaching partner and I
are in the process of developing our Middle East unit. We stumbled across a book by Moshe Safdie, an architect whose acclaim for
Habitat, an affordable housing project that he designed for World
Expo '67 in Montreal, earned him many commissions in Jerusalem.
In his introduction to *Jerusalem, the Future and the Past* (Houghton
Mifflin, 1989), he presented the problem with which he had grappled when drawing up designs for this ancient city: How do I
build something that is true to the present as well as the past? My
partner and I saw the perfect entry point. All children have experience with buildings and living spaces. With some introductory activities to get them thinking about these places with a greater
awareness of architecture, form, and function, along with a week
of gathering and reading newspaper articles on the Middle East to
establish what we know and don't understand about the region,
we will ask them to design a structure that addresses Safdie's question. We envision the exploration of the Middle East, past and present, unfolding from there.

As I read the previous chapters, I am struck by the similarities between these teachers' journeys in developing curriculum for their
classes and my own journey. None of us returned to our classes
with the intent of replicating our experiences with Bill Saturno and
the Maya curriculum seminar. We all had our own professional

histories to build upon, our own school structures to contend with, our own students to focus on. Yet we all started with the high standards that had been inspired by our time with Bill: Are we setting our students up to gain real understanding of the people we are studying? Are we creating opportunities for curiosity to inspire them and problems to compel them into wanting to learn more? Will they finish the unit looking at their world and themselves in a new light? I do not believe that we all took this approach because of who we are. Rather, I believe that the structure of the curriculum seminar set us off on our journeys well supplied with our own experiences in learning and thinking about what we would eventually ask our students to study. Professional development opportunities need to provide for teachers as the curriculum seminars provided for us. Think of the possibilities for schools when teachers create museums together, work with artists, examine primary sources, and talk with field experts and each other in the process. By going through experiences, teachers will have grappled with the logistics of ambitious group projects, and they will know that they can be done. Teachers will demand firsthand knowledge. They know that a local artist can be a living resource who can help to build a deep knowledge base. They will design field trips to museums that are closer to on-site excavations than tours. Their time spent negotiating the choices entailed in their own exhibitions will reassure them as their own students argue over similar questions. They will not rush in to smooth the waters. Most importantly, they will have had the luxury of professional redevelopment with colleagues from diverse communities—and will leave richer for the access to the range of resources and experience. These are the kinds of experiences that make it possible for teachers to explore what they need to teach, experiences that recognize the real need for models, not scripts.

Notes

1. An excellent source for primary documents on African-American history is *Crossing the Danger Water, Three Hundred Years of African-American Writing*, ed. Deidre Mullane. 1993. Anchor Books, Doubleday.

2. *Fun with Chinese Characters*, in *The Straits Times Collection* (Singapore: Federal Publications, 1980), is an excellent resource for activities like this, for it has easily reproducible pages that explore the origin of a rich range of characters.
3. Pali is an ancient religious language in India, and the *Pali Canon* is believed to be the first written record of the teachings of the Buddha.
4. Tan, Amy. 1989. *The Joy Luck Club*. Ballantine Books, New York.

Appendix: Maya Adult Bibliography

Compiled by Harvard University Museums of Cultural and Natural History

Westerners have been fascinated by the ancient Maya for over 150 years. In that time, knowledge and thoughts about these people have changed considerably. In the past twenty years, the increasing ability to read the Maya writing system (among other things) has led to a radically different view of the Maya than before—they have metamorphosed into a densely populated, warlike culture ruled by kings whose names and deeds are known. Therefore, any book or article published before the mid 1970s is likely to be very out of sync with current thought. These books are still prevalent in libraries, and are therefore listed here, but should be used with a great deal of caution, if at all. It is especially important for students to understand and be able to recognize changes in scholarship and ideas as they do research. Remember, just because something is said in a book does not mean it is right. The same warning could well be given for the more current books in this bibliography. They will be outdated in time too. No book can replace a critically questioning mind when approaching a new field of inquiry.

Anderson, Marilyn and Jonathan Garlock. 1988. *Granddaughters of Corn, Portraits of Guatemalan Women*. Willimantic, Conn. Curbstone Press.
> Photographs of Guatemalan women with first-person accounts of the everyday reality experienced by women in Guatemala, during years of violence and repression that brought the term *los desapareci-dos* (the disappeared); a book that is both artful and important to human rights.

Carmack, Robert M. 1981. *The Quiche Mayas of Utatlan*. Norman: University of Oklahoma Press.
> An account of the Quiches who created a powerful Maya kingdom in the highlands of Guatemala shortly before the Spanish conquest. Carmack incorporates the known archaeology, the existing chronicles of the Quiches, and surviving elements of their culture in what

is our most comprehensive account of the history and traditions of the Quiche people.

Coe, Michael. 1987. *The Maya*. New York: Thames and Hudson.

A highly readable account of Maya civilization, it is also readily available.

———. 1991. *Breaking the Maya Code*. New York: Thames and Hudson.

Tells the story of the latest breakthrough in deciphering Maya glyphs. A detective story told by a renowned Maya scholar who has known many of the major "characters." It was a Book of the Month Club selection.

Everton, Macduff. 1991. *The Modern Maya: A Culture in Transition*. Albuquerque: University of New Mexico Press.

Sensitive photographs and personal experiences in Central America today.

Fash, William. 1991. *Scribes, Warriors and Kings: the City of Copan and the Ancient Maya*. New York: Thames and Hudson.

One of the most important of Maya cities, many artifacts from early excavations of this site are in Harvard's Peabody Museum.

Fussell, Betty. 1992. *The Story of Corn: The Myths and History, the Culture and Agriculture, the Art and Science of America's Quintessential Crop*. New York: Alfred K. Knopf.

The title says it all and the book delivers what it promises.

Gallencamp, Charles, and R. E. Johnson, ed. 1985. *Maya: Treasures of an Ancient Civilization*. New York: Harry N. Abrams.

This catalogue accompanied an exhibit at the Museum of Natural History in New York. It includes an informative text and many photographs, both in color and black and white, of artifacts collected for this exhibition.

Hammond, Norman. 1990. *Ancient Maya Civilization*. New Jersey: Rutgers University Press.

An excellent and widely used archaeology textbook of the rise and fall of the Maya, including sections on politics, social structure, land use, trade and architecture. Maps included; black and white photographs.

Henderson, John S. 1981. *The World of the Ancient Maya*. Ithaca, N.Y.; Cornell University Press.

A comprehensive account of Maya cultural tradition from its earliest roots to Spanish conquest. It clearly explains the distinct lowland and highland ecologies and peoples, Maya calendars, and the complex Maya pantheon.

Jones, Christopher. 1984. *Deciphering Maya Hieroglyphics*. University Museum, Philadelphia: University of Pennsylvania.

Contains a great deal of detailed information on recognizing glyphs, on the three cycle counts, on calculating in Maya, etc. A great resource.

Marks, Copeland. 1985. *False Tongues and Sunday Bread: A Guatemalan Cookbook*. New York: M. Evans.
   Maya cookery.
Menchu, Rigoberta. 1984. *I, Rigoberta Menchu: An Indian Woman in Guatemala*. New York: Verso.
   The author is a Mayan woman who has organized and fought back against extreme government repression of her people. Her life and work, detailed in this autobiography, won her the Nobel Peace Prize for 1992. An English translation of her work.
Miller, Mary Ellen. 1986. *The Art of Mesoamerica from Olmec to Aztec*. London: Thames and Hudson.
   And the Maya come in the middle—a widely available and relatively readable book from an art historian's perspective.
Montejo, Victor. *Testimony: Death of a Guatemalan Village*, trans. Victor Perera. Willimantic, CT: Curbstone Press.
   An eyewitness account by a Guatemalan primary school teacher, detailing a specific violent conflict between the indigenous Mayan people and the army.
Morris, Walter F. 1987 *Living Maya*. New York: Harry N. Abrams.
   Photographs and text explore the Maya today through their stunning embroidered and woven textiles. It focuses exceptionally strongly on women.
Omang, Joanne. 1992. *Incident at Akabal*. Boston: Houghton Mifflin.
   A powerful, moving novel about a Central American village at a point of crisis.
Otto-Diniz, Sara. 1986. *Mysteries of Maya*. New York: Harry N. Abrams.
   This catalogue of a museum exhibit includes geographical area occupied by the Maya, a time line, historical indicators, art symbolism, tombs, and burial customs, cities, warriors, and the sacred cenote. The photographs are excellent and extensively captioned.
Perera, Victor, and Robert D. Bruce. 1982. *The Last Lords of Palenque: The Lacandon Mayas of the Mexican Rain Forest*. Boston: Little, Brown and Co.
   The Lacandon follow a very traditional lifestyle today.
Reader's Digest Association. 1986. *Mysteries of the Ancient Americas*. Pleasantville, N.Y.: Reader's Digest.
   This book, with one chapter on the Maya, seems well written and generously illustrated with photographs. In the Reader's Digest style, the writing can be sensationalist, but it is straightforward and easy to read.
Schele, Linda, and Mary Ellen Miller. 1986. *Blood of Kings*. New York: William Morrow.
   A wonderful, rather "free" account of Maya "history" as it is now being revealed by the acceleration in glyph translation.
Stephens, John L. 1969. *Incidents of Travel in Central America, Chiapas and Yucatan*. Dover Publications. London: A. Hall, Virtue & Co. 1854.

Republication of 1841 edition with additional material from a 1954 edition, in two New York volumes. An account of two expeditions to Mexico and Central America in 1839 and 1841. This book introduced the ancient Maya to the rest of the world and is still fascinating reading.

Stuart, George, and Gene S. Stuart. 1977. The Mysterious Maya. Washington D.C.: National Geographic Society.

Another book by National Geographic's top archaeologists on the Maya. It does not reflect the most recent discoveries on the ancient Maya but is, of course, easily available in libraries.

———. 1993. *Lost Kingdoms of the Maya*. Washington D.C.: National Geographic Society.

The most up-to-date of National Geographic's many Maya books came out in conjunction with their television special in the winter of 1993.

Tedlock, Dennis, (trans). 1985. *Popul Vuh: The Definitive Edition of the Mayan Book of the Dawn of Life and the Glories of Gods and Kings*. New York: Simon and Schuster.

———. 1993. *Breath on the Mirror: Mythic Voices and Visions of the Living Maya*. San Francisco: Harper.

A stunning book, it portrays the continuity of the stories from past to present Maya and their current use.

Thompson, J. Eric S. 1966. *The Rise and Fall of Maya Civilization*. Norman: Oklahoma University Press.

A comprehensive and scholarly work on the Maya. Thompson was the preeminent archaeologist of "last generation." His work does not reflect the advances in reading glyphs or understanding the nature of Maya warfare, but is vital to the development of Maya studies and is frequently found in libraries.

———. 1970. *Maya History and Religion*. Norman: Oklahoma University Press.

Again, this and other books by the famed archaeologist are readily available in libraries, but they reflect out of date theories. The Maya are no longer considered a peaceful, nonwarlike people.

———. 1975. *Maya Archaeologist*. Norman: Oklahoma University Press.

Thompson's autobiography, it is an account of excavations of ancient Maya cities and of his contacts with the descendants of their inhabitants. The caveat above applies here too. A paperback edition came out in 1990.

Time-Life Books. 1993. *The Magnificent Maya*. Alexandria, VA: Time-Life Books.

A copiously illustrated and up-to-date book in their new *Lost Civilizations* series, it is suprisingly unsensationalistic (unlike the companion volume on the Aztec), but that only a single page is devoted to the contemporary Maya is a disgrace.

Weaver, Muriel. 1981. *The Aztecs, Maya, and their Predecessors.* New York: Academic Press.

> The author wrote the book to supply a single volume that will cover the archaeology of both central Mexico and the Maya area. Weaver makes a successful attempt in this book to fit synthesis and generalizations into a comprehensive framework of pre-Columbian history. Excellent, very readable book for obtaining a sense of the separate and interrelated identities of Mesoamerican cultural traditions.

Films, Videos, and Slides

The Chinampas. Anne Prutzman. University of California Extension Center for Media and Independent Learning.

> The Maya and others used this sustainable system of aquatic agriculture. This video looks at the surviving Chinampa farmers of Mexico City. Available through the University of California Extension Center for Media and Independent Learning, 2176 Shatuck Ave., Berkeley, CA 94704. Telephone: 510-642-0460, Fax: 510-643-8683.

Daughters of Ixchel: Maya Tread of Change. Kathryn Lipke Vigesaa and John McKay. University of California Extension Center for Media and Independent Learning.

> Focuses on Guatemalan weavers and their changing yet enduring traditions.

Guatemalan Women: Weaving, Repression and Resistance. Marilyn Anderson, producer.

> See the book (in bibliography) by Anderson. Available through Mayan Crafts, Inc. 845 No. Lincoln St., Arlington, VA 22201.

History of the Mayas and Other Indigenous Groups of Central America. Project Crossroads.

> Slides and narration give an overview of the history and daily life of Central America's indigenous peoples, with speculation about the Maya "collapse." Available for $32.10 through Project Crossroads, P.O. Box 1963, Santa Fe, NM 87505-1963.

Last of the Mayas. Syracuse University, 28 minutes.

> Available through Syracuse University. Telephone: 315-423-2452; Fax: 800-223 2409.

The Living Maya. 1995. University of California Extension Center for Media and Independent Learning.

> Four hour-long programs document traditional and contemporary forces in a Yucatan village today. In English, Spanish, and Maya with English subtitles.

Legacy: Central America: The Burden of Time. Michael Wood, host.

> Reveals how ancient cultures continue to influence our lives today. Focuses primarily on Maya, but includes the Inca (who were not in Central America) and the Aztec (who were).

Maya of Ancient and Modern Yucatan. Syracuse University, 22 minutes.
Mayaland (Central America). Syracuse University, 40 minutes.
Maya Lords of the Jungle. WGBH Television, Boston. Color, 52 minutes.
Broadcast on December 29, 1981, in the "Odyssey" series.
MayaQuest: The Mystery Trail. 1995. MECC, 6160 Summit Dr., North Minneapolis, MN.
Mayans, Apolcaypse Then. Syracuse University, 26 minutes.
Mexican Indian Legends. Syracuse University, 17 minutes.
Popul Vuh: The Creation Myth of the Maya. 1989. Patricia Amlin, producer. University of California Extension Center for Media and Independent Learning.
> This beautifully animated version of the famous sixteenth-century. Mayan tale draws on ancient Mayan art to tell of the creation of the world. It replicates the somewhat confusing nature of the tale and should be viewed only after students know the basic storyline, but it should definitely be watched.

Time-Life's Lost Civilizations: Maya—Blood of Kings, prod. and dir. Joe Westbrook, 48 min., Time-Life, 1994, videocassette.

Journal Articles

Angier, N. 1981. "New Clues to the Maya Mystery." *Discover* (June 2).
> An illustrated account of how archaeologists are unearthing the city of El Mirador. It also depicts Copán and other Maya sites.

Kinoshita, J. 1990. "Maya Art for the Record." *Scientific American* (August).
> Examines the condition under which the ancient Maya murals of Bonampak ("original" copies of which can be seen at Harvard's Peabody Museum) are deteriorating and the attempt to save them.

Lemonick, M. D. 1993. "Lost Secrets of the Maya." *Time* (August 9).
> Somewhat sensationalistic account of recent Maya discoveries. Use with caution, keeping a sharp eye out for the stereotypes of both the Maya and the women (especially) who study them today.

Author unknown. 1991. "Mayans, Hawaiians, Tibetans." *Whole Earth Review* 72.
> If you can find this, it contains articles and references to books and videos on the contemporary Mayas, including one article on a study group about the *Popul Vuh*, creation myth of the Maya. Contact *Whole Earth Review* at P.O. Box 38, Sausalito, CA 94966-9932.

Archaeology

This magazine is focused on archaeology throughout the world and is written for the popular audience. It should be available in most public libraries. Older students may be aware of it. The following articles are from it.

Coe, M. 1991. "Triumph of the Spirit." September/October.
    Coe knows Yuri Knorosov, the Russian linguist whose work, described here, initiated the modern breakthrough in Maya glyph translation.
Griffin, G. 1991. "A Most Happy Mayanist." September/October.
    This article is about Linda Schele, an exuberant art historian whose work (see elsewhere in this bibliography) is transforming the current understanding of the ancient Maya.
Hammond, N. 1983. "The Discovery of Tikal." May/June.
Healy, P. F. 1988. "Music of the Maya." January/February.
Jackson, L., and H. McKillop. 1987. "Maya Trade at Wild Cane Cay, Belize." February.
Schaffer, A. 1992. "On the Edge of the Maya World." March/April.
Schele, L., and M. E. Miller. "The Blood of Kings: A New Interpretation of Maya Art." May/June.
    This article introduces the exhibit to which the book *Blood of Kings* (see bibliography) is a companion volume.

National Geographic

All students and teachers are aware of this invaluable resource, for both its well-written articles and its superb photography. For many decades, it has particularly focused on the ancient Maya and should be one of the first stops in any student research. Here are a few of its Maya articles. Just don't limit yourself to only using this magazine.

Adams, R. E. 1986. "Rio Azul." March.
Fasquelle, R., and W. L. Fash Jr. 1989. "Copán: A Royal Tomb Discovered." October.
    This details the unearthing of a Maya nobleman's tomb.
Garret, W. E. 1989. "La Ruta Maya." October.
    Traces Maya culture and outlines a plan for a 1,500-mile tour encircling the Maya realm. A double map of Maya lands included.
Mathery, R. T. 1987. "El Mirador: An Early Maya Metropolis Uncovered." September.
    Description of Mayan city now believed to be the oldest and largest of the civilization. Includes map, illustrations, and photographs.
Stuart, G. 1989. "City of Kings and Commoners: New Discoveries at Copán in Western Honduras." October.
    Stuart put forth ideas to explain the mysterious collapse of the Maya capital in the ninth century A.D.
Stuart, G. 1992. "Maya Heartland Under Seige." November.

Curriculum Resources

Baktun. 1988. Chicago: Associates in Multicultural and International Education.

Batz'l K'op (True Speech). 1988. Chicago: Associates in Multicultural and International Education.

Bolon. 1988. Chicago: Associates in Multicultural and International Education.

> The above three curriculum books for students are available through Associates in Multicultural and International Education, P.O. Box 14256, Chicago, IL 60614.

Directory of Central America Classroom Resources. Minneapolis: Central America Resource Center.

> Covers grades K–12 and has curricula, audiovisuals, supplemental resources, organizations, and directories. Available through the Central America Resource Center, 317 17th Avenue, S.E. Minneapolis, MN 55414-2077; telephone: 612-627-9445.

Mayan Calendrics. Berkeley: Dolphin Software.

> In addition to having three calendars—the long count, the tzolkin, and the haab—the Maya further complicated matters by occasionally shifting the haab one or two days in relation to the tzolkin. Available through Dolphin Software, 48 Shattuck Sq., #147, Berkeley, CA 94704, for $68.00 on $5^{1}/_{4}$ or $3^{1}/_{2}$ inch disk in MS-DOS 3.0 format.

Folk Tales from Central America. Santa Fe: Project Crossroads.

> Collection of folktales that includes a wide selection from the seven Central American countries. These include historic (Spanish, Caribbean, and Mayan), humorous (Tio Conejo) and moral tales. Available for $3.00 through Project Crossroads, P.O. Box 1963, Santa Fe, NM 87505-1963.

The Second Voyage of the Mimi. 1989. Sunburst Communications.

> An extensive curriculum designed for schools. It involves written, video, and computer materials and looks at the Maya both past and present.

Smith, A. 1992. *Mayan Safari: A Beginning Spanish Reader*. White Plains, NY: Longman Spanish Culture Series.

Voris, H., et al. 1986. *Teach the Mind, Touch the Spirit: A Guide to Focused Field Trips*. Chicago: Department of Education, Field Museum of Natural History.

> This publication is an invaluable resource when planning a trip to any museum. It clearly explains techniques and the reasoning behind them for a successful trip and learning experience.

Maya Bibliography for Students

Ashabronner, B. 1986. *Children of the Maya: A Guatemalan Indian Odyssey*. Dodd, Mead.

> Background on the political dynamics behind genocide of the Mayan Indians at the hands of the Guatemalan army. Stories told by survivors of village massacres, experience of refugees through

Mexico and their resettlement in Indiantown, Florida, a migrant worker population center. Grades 5 and up.

Baker, B. 1965. *Walk the World's Rim*. New York: Harper & Row.
Available in libraries, but outdated.

Beck, B. 1983. *The Ancient Maya*. New York: Franklin Watts.
Description of Mayan origins, details of everyday life, clothing, body decoration, cooking, Mayan traditions. Highland and lowland Maya are generalized into "the Maya," which tends to ignore differences of people living in environmentally distinct areas. Interestingly written, good independent reading for upper elementary or middle school students.

Bierhorst, J., ed. 1986. *The Monkey's Haircut and Other Stories Told by the Maya*. Morrow.
A collection of twenty-two stories, some of which are from ancient traditions, some of which reflect the influx of Western Europeans traditions on Mexican folktales. Introduction points out how tales reflect the customs and beliefs of the Maya people. Grades 4 and up.

Bleeker, S. 1961. *The Maya: Indians of Central America*. New York: Morrow Junior Books.
This book is part of an extensive but now outdated series on Native Americans that is found in most libraries.

Brandt, K. 1985. *Mexico and Central America*. Troll Associates.
Compares and contrasts modern nations and ancient empires of Mexico and Central America. Includes geography and topography, descriptions of their sophisticated societies, the Feathered Serpent Legend, and its consequences to the arrival of the Spanish conquest. Grades 3 and up.

Gifford, D. 1983. *Warriors, Gods and Spirits from Central and South American Mythology*. New York: Schocken Books.
Myths and legends of the Mayas, Toltecs, Aztecs, and Incas, with exceptionally beautiful illustrations. It includes a retelling of the *Popul Vuh*. For all ages.

Greene, J. 1992. *The Maya*. Franklin Watts.
Part of the *A First Book* series, this is not a bad book for later elementary age readers and up. It has a great deal of information but presents everything as "fact," without discussing sources or the possibility that something may be an (educated) guess by archaeologists.

Karen, R. 1972. *Song of the Quail*. New York: Four Winds Press.
Comprehensive, well-organized and -written history that presents a wide range of information. Two fictionalized stories are included. Also includes many clear photos of Mayan designs, pottery, and sculpted figures. There is a bibliography and a glossary and a list of Mayan sites and museum collections. It does not reflect more recent discoveries.

Karlovich, R. A. 1985. *Rise Up in Anger—Latin America Today*. New York: Julian Messner.

Helpful for presenting political, economic, and historical background for students on Latin America.

Macauley, D. 1979. *The Motel of the Mysteries.* Boston: Houghton Mifflin.

This book is not about the Maya themselves, but cleverly and amusingly imagines what future archaeologists might make of our own culture.

McKissack, P. S. 1985. *The Maya.* Chicago: The Children's Press.

For younger readers. History, language, customs, culture, religions, and warfare of the ancient Central American civilization of the Maya. Contains at least one glaring error: the *Popul Vuh* is described as a game rather than as a myth. It is available in English or Spanish.

Meyer, C., and C. Gallenkamp. 1985. *The Mystery of the Ancient Maya*. New York: Atheneum.

Well written book introducing Mayan civilizations by telling the story of two explorers, John Stephens and Frederick Catherwood, who traveled to Central America in the mid-1800s. The work of other early archaeologists is also described: Edward Thompson began work in 1885 and Sylvanus Morley in 1912. Useful illustrations. Grades 6 and up.

Montejo, V. 1991. *The Bird Who Cleans the World and Other Mayan Fables*. Willimantic, CT: Curbstone Press.

Collected and translated from Jakaltek Mayan language. Twenty-one languages are still spoken in Guatemala. Folktales deal with themes of creation, nature, mutual respect, ethnic relations, and conflicts. Grades 4 and up.

NECA (Network Educators on Central America) 1988. *Where Is Guatemala and What Is Quetzal?*

The culture and experience of indigenous Guatemalans is compared and contrasted to those of the native peoples of North America. It includes geographic information and a resource guide. Junior high. Available through NECA, 1118 22nd St. N.W., Washington, DC 20037.

Nougier, L. 1985. *The Days of the Maya, Aztecs and Incas*. New York: Silver Burdett.

Moderate to advanced text but engaging format; mostly colorful illustrations with captions. The book is set up by category—from boatsmen and hunter to cooking, pottery making, working with stone; games to temples.

O'Dell, S. 1983. *The Captive; The Feathered Serpent; The Amethyst Ring*. Boston: Houghton Mifflin.

This trilogy tells the story of a young Jesuit seminarian who fights against the enslavement of conquest of Central America. The story takes one from Spain to Mexico, Central America, and further south to Machu Pichu. Well-written and -researched, as is normal for O'Dell.

Odijk, P. 1983. *The Mayas.* New York: Silver Burdett.
> From the series *The Ancient World*, Grades 5 and up.

Perl, L. 1982. *Guatemala—Central America's Living Past.* New York: William Morrow and Co.
> Excellent description of the topography and the climate of Guatemala. Includes history of the Mayas in that country, the Spanish conquest, and culture and contemporary Guatemala. Very informative with many photographs.

Pine, T. S. and J. Levine. 1971. *The Maya Knew.* McGraw Hill: New York.
> A book designed for younger and less able readers. Format includes information about Mayan civilization, comparing it to our own culture, and suggestions for things to make on a given topic. It is written in easy-to-understand language.

Price, C. 1972. *Heirs of the Ancient Maya: A Portrait of the Lacandon Indians.* New York: Charles Scribner and Sons.
> A great deal of information is presented here through the text and through photos by Gertrude Duby Blom. Vocabulary supports the curriculum.

Rehmer, H. and M. Anchondo. *Mexico: How We Came to the Fifth World.*
> Bilingual Spanish/English; full color. This is the myth of ancient Mexico that tells us how the world evolved through four previous worlds. Illustrations based on the original Indian picture writings. Ages 7–12.

Roy. C. 1972. *The Serpent and the Sun: Myths of the Mexican World.* New York: Farrar, Straus and Giroux.
> Included two Maya myths from the *Popul Vuh*, as well as Aztec stories.

Sexton, J. D. 1992. *Mayan Folktales: Folklore from Lake Atitlan, Guatemala.* New York: Doubleday.
> A collection of stories, dance dramas, and others collected today.

Sherrow, V. 1994. *The Maya Indians.* New York: Chelsea House Publishers.
> Well-written book for good readers in late elementary grades and up. It contains excellent chapters on the Spanish Conquest and the Maya today, including an extensive discussion on the tragic situation in Guatemala.

Shetterly, S. H. 1990. *The Dwarf-Wizard of Uxmal.* New York: Atheneum.
> A read-aloud picture book that casts the David and Goliath theme into a Mayan legend; the author found recorded in a book written by the nineteenth-century American explorer Robert Stephens. Set in the Yucatan peninsula, the story contains magic, humor, and determination.

Smith, E. L. 1983. *Mexico: Giant of the South.* Minneapolis: Dillon Press.
> Contents include fast facts about Mexico, cultural ways and customs, growth and change over a 3,000-year history, legends, celebrations, and family life. Grade 5 and up.

Sutton, M. 1967. *Among the Maya Ruins.* Chicago: Rand McNally.
> This book describes the adventures of two early European explorers. A good narrative on what it was like 100 years ago to discover virtually unknown sites such as Copán. Catherwood's and Stephen's lives make interesting reading.

Trout, L. 1989. *The Maya: Middle America.* New York: Chelsea House.
> This book has snuck into the excellent *Indians of North America* series, and one can be glad of it. Well-researched and -illustrated, it presents the ancient Maya and not just the "facts" on these people. Grades 5 and up.

Volkmer, J. A. 1990. *Song of the Chirimia.* Minneapolis: Carolrhoda Books.
> This picture book is a retelling of a Guatemalan folktalke. The illustrations are based on Mayan stone carvings.

Von Hagen, V. 1960. *Maya—Lane of the Turkey and the Deer.* New York: World Publishing.
> A decently written book presenting the ancient Maya through a fictionalized story. It is a pity that it is out of date.

Weaver, M. P. 1981. *The Aztecs, Maya and Their Predecessors.* New York: Academic Press (Harcourt Brace Jovanovich).

Whitlock, R. 1976. *Everyday Life of the Maya.* New York: G. Putnam & Son.

Wisniewski, D. 1991. *The Rain Player.* New York: Clarion Books.
> Gorgeous cut paper illustrations depict this fictional story of a Maya ball game.

Yoder, C. 1985. "The Maya Civilization." *Faces: The Magazine About People.* Cobblestone Publishing Co. Vol. 2 (2).
> Short articles for children on various aspects of the ancient Maya.

Coloring Books

Coloring Book of Incas, Aztecs and Mayas. Santa Barbara: Bellerophon Books.
> Don't sneer at coloring books when dealing with the ancient Maya. Their sense of design and filling of space is very different from our own culture's and can be very confusing when first viewed. Line drawings such as those in this book and the others below clarify an initially confusing picture. Letting students examine and color in these illustrations familiarizes them with the conventions of Mayan art before they look at the original thing.

Caraway, C. 1981. *The Mayan Design Book.* Owing Mills, MD: Stemmer House.

Turner, W.C. 1980. *Maya Design Coloring Book.* New York: Dover Publications, Inc.
> Photocopyable full-page authentic Maya designs, each one identified and its purpose and meaning described at the bottom of the page. Alas, it is out of print. Snag a copy if you can find it.

Contributors

Marg Costello teaches seventh-grade language arts and social studies at Horace Mann Academic Middle School in the Mission District of San Francisco, CA. She is chair of the social studies department and a mentor teacher.

Victoria Rodríguez Garvey is a teacher at Alexis I. duPont Middle School in Wilmington, DE. Mrs. Garvey teaches all subjects to a self-contained bilingual education classroom. She has been involved in PACE and New Standards Project and was A.I.'s Teacher of the Year for 1996–1997.

Tammy Swales Metzler is a teacher at Thomas Jefferson Middle School in Rochester, NY. She has been involved with PACE for several years. Ms. Swales Metzler is currently functioning as a teacher-on-assignment, developing the Jefferson Portfolio Assessment System as well as other curricular initiatives for students and teachers.

Miriam Nason teaches sixth-grade humanities at O'Farrell Community School in San Diego, CA. She has long been interested in ancient civilizations and shares this interest with her students through her teaching.

Phyllis McDonough Rado has been teaching Language Arts in middle school for over twenty years (and she still appears sane). She is currently teaching seventh-grade language arts at Alexis I. duPont Middle School in Wilmington, DE. She has been involved with PACE and the New Standards Project.

Shannon Thomas teaches humanities to sixth graders at O'Farrell Community School in San Diego, CA. Among his primary goals are to encourage his students to ask interesting and probing questions and to respond with equally interesting answers.